Set design by Adrianne Lobel

Photo by Joan Marcus

A scene from the Broadway production of *The Diary of Anne Frank*.

THE DIARY OF ANNE FRANK

BY **FRANCES GOODRICH**
AND **ALBERT HACKETT**

NEWLY ADAPTED BY
WENDY KESSELMAN

★ **Definitive Edition 2016**

★

DRAMATISTS
PLAY SERVICE
INC.

for Brian

ACKNOWLEDGMENTS

With special thanks to:

Brian Briody, Chris Burney, Grayson Covil, Anne Dobbs, Myra Dorrell, Deborah Dwork, Buddy and Gerti Elias, Bloeme Evers-Emden, Michael Q. Fellmeth, Bob Fennell, Miep Gies, Carol Gilligan, Maria Goudsblom-Oestreicher, Dienke Hondius, Elisabeth Kashey, Hedda Kopf, Tina Landau, George P. Lane, Lawrence L. Langer, James Lapine, Elaine McIlroy, Father John Neiman, Anna Ornstein, Rosalind Pace, Jack and Ina Polak, Alvin Rosenfeld, Dan Moses Schreier, Jo Seelman, Maureen Shea, Dineke Stam, Haleh Roshan Stilwell, Emma Strauss, Maurice and Netty Vanderpol, Bret Verb, and Dora and Jules Zaidenweber.

AUTHOR'S NOTE

If artistically desirable, the play may be performed without an intermission. Alternatively the play may be performed with an intermission, leaving the actors onstage.

Close attention should be paid to the moments when Anne speaks directly to us and when she is heard voiceover.

It is strongly recommended that actors avoid using Dutch or German accents. The effect of such accents is not to enhance authenticity but to diminish it. By the same token, an effort should be made to properly pronounce foreign words and phrases that appear in the play, including the names of the concentration camps in Mr. Frank's last monologue. (Also, please note that the first syllable in "Putti" is pronounced like the first syllable in "pudding.") For additional context, at the back of this volume is a glossary of translations into English from the German and Hebrew that is used in the play.

The author recommends that the historical sound material and sound effects compiled by Dan Moses Schreier for the Broadway production be used in connection with productions of the play. Please see the Sound Effects page for further information.

In the final powerful image of the Broadway production, projections of Anne's words were cast over the stage, onto the walls and ceiling of the theatre. If this proves impossible, it is desirable to cast her words onto the stage itself.

Wendy Kesselman's adaptation of THE DIARY OF ANNE FRANK was produced on Broadway by David Stone, Amy Nederlander-Case, Jon B. Platt, Jujamcyn Theatres and Hal Luftig, in association with Harriet Newman Leve and James D. Stern, at the Music Box Theatre in December 1997. It was directed by James Lapine; the set design was by Adrianne Lobel; the lighting design was by Brian MacDevitt; the sound design was by Dan Moses Schreier; the costume design was by Martin Pakledinaz; and the production stage manager was David Hyslop. The cast was as follows:

ANNE FRANK	Natalie Portman
OTTO FRANK	George Hearn
EDITH FRANK	Sophie Hayden
MARGOT FRANK	Missy Yager
MIEP GIES	Jessica Walling
PETER VAN DAAN	Jonathan Kaplan
MR. KRALER	Philip Goodwin
MRS. VAN DAAN	Linda Lavin
MR. VAN DAAN	Harris Yulin
MR. DUSSEL	Austin Pendleton
FIRST MAN	Peter Kybart
SECOND MAN	James Hallet
THIRD MAN	Eddie Kaye Thomas

CHARACTERS

(in order of appearance)

ANNE FRANK

OTTO FRANK

EDITH FRANK

MARGOT FRANK

MIEP GIES

PETER VAN DAAN

MR. KRALER

MRS. VAN DAAN

MR. VAN DAAN

MR. DUSSEL

FIRST MAN

SECOND MAN

THIRD MAN

SETTING

The play takes place in the top floors of the annex to an office building in Amsterdam, Holland, during the years of World War II.

THE DIARY OF ANNE FRANK

ACT ONE

Darkness. The sound of marching feet. In the distance, coming closer, loud voices sing:

> Ihr Sturmsoldaten jung und alt,
> nehmt die Waffen in die Hand
> Denn der Jude hauset fürchterlich
> Im deutschen Vaterland
>
> Wenn Sturmsoldaten in Schlacht 'rein zieht
> ja dann hat er frohen Mut
> Wenn das Judenblut vom Messer spritzt
> ja geht's noch mal so gut!

The sound of seagulls. The sound of pouring rain. The Westertoren clock chimes six.

Footsteps approach.

Within the darkness, we dimly perceive several people moving up a steep wooden staircase. Silence.

A shaft of light comes up on a yellow Star of David, with the black inscription "Jood," on Anne's coat.

The light opens up slowly to reveal a stylized tableau of the Frank family huddled together, their hair wet, their dark coats soaked with rain. Over the left breast of each — the yellow Star.

For a moment the Franks cling to each other, then separate, slowly begin to take off their drenched clothes. Each of them — Anne, Margot, Edith, and Otto Frank — wear many layers. On every coat, jacket, vest, raincoat, sweater, dress, another yellow Star is revealed.

Light comes up further to reveal the Franks' hiding place — the Annex — crammed to the ceiling with cardboard boxes, piles of bedding, assorted furniture.

Overwhelmed, Edith Frank collapses on a couch. Margot takes off her glasses, lies on a bare mattress on the floor. Excited, Anne runs around exploring, as Otto Frank opens a carton of sheets and pillows. The light slowly brightens. Anne and her father, in stylized actions, unpack cartons, arrange furniture, making the Annex into a home, as, numbed, Edith and Margot lie silent, not moving, their eyes open wide. Anne gently lays a blanket over Margot.

Throughout, voiceover, we hear Anne reading from her diary.

ANNE. *(V.O.)* July sixth, 1942. A few days ago, Father began to talk about going into hiding. He said it would be very hard for us to live cut off from the rest of the world. He sounded so serious I felt scared. "Don't worry, Anneke. Just enjoy your carefree life while you can." Carefree? I was born in Frankfort on June twelfth, 1929. Because we're Jewish, my father emigrated to Holland in 1933. He heard Hitler's marching gangs sing that horrible song, "when Jew-blood spurts from the knife," and knew it was time to leave. But Hitler invaded Holland on May tenth, 1940. Five days later the Dutch surrendered, the Germans arrived — and the trouble started for the Jews. *(A pause.)*

Father was forced to give up his business — manufacturing products used to make jam. We couldn't use streetcars, couldn't go to the theatre or movies anymore, couldn't be out on the *street* after 8 P.M., couldn't even sit in our own gardens! We had to turn in our bicycles. No beaches, no swimming pools, no libraries — we couldn't even walk on the sunny side of the streets! Our identity cards were stamped with a big black "J." And ... we had to wear the yellow star. But somehow life went on. Until yesterday. A call-up notice from the SS! My sister Margot was ordered to report for work in Germany, to the Westerbork transit camp. A call-up — everyone knows what that means! *(She pauses.)*

At five-thirty this morning, we closed the door of our apartment behind us. My cat was the only living creature I said goodbye to. The unmade beds, the breakfast things on the table all created the impression we'd left in a hurry. *(A pause.)*

And our destination? We walked two and a half miles in the pouring rain all the way to … 263 Prinsengracht — father's office building! Our hiding place, the "Secret Annex," is right behind it upstairs. Even though the Germans forced Father out, he still runs the office with Mr. Kraler and Miep, who've offered to help us while we're in hiding. *(As Mr. Frank pulls a large tarpaulin off the kitchen table, he sees a rat move across the floor. Mrs. Frank shrieks.)*

MRS. FRANK. A rat!

MR. FRANK. Shhh! *(He motions her to be quiet as Miep comes up the steps.)* Ah, Miep!

MIEP. Mr. Frank. Thank God you arrived safely.

ANNE. *(Running to embrace her.)* Miep!

MIEP. Anne. *(Margot and Mrs. Frank slowly sit up.)* Mrs. Frank, Margot — you must be exhausted. If only we'd known, we would have had it all ready for you.

MR. FRANK. You've done too much already, Miep. Besides, it's good for us to keep busy. As you see, Anne's my little helper.

MIEP. I see that. *(She looks down the steps where Peter van Daan, a shy, awkward boy of sixteen, wearing a heavy coat with the conspicuous yellow star, waits nervously. He is carrying a cat in a basket.)* Peter — come in!

MR. FRANK. *(Quickly coming forward, shaking his hand.)* Welcome, Peter. Peter van Daan, children.

ANNE. *(Rushing toward him.)* Welcome to the Annex!

MR. FRANK. Peter — this is Anne. Margot. And my wife, Mrs. Frank.

PETER. *(Solemnly shaking hands with Mrs. Frank.)* Mrs. Frank.

MRS. FRANK. Forgive me, Peter. I'm not quite myself. But I'm glad you'll be with us.

MARGOT. I am too.

ANNE. *(Looking down at the basket.)* A cat! *(Turning to Margot.)* He has a cat!

PETER. *(Self-conscious.)* A black one.

ANNE. We have a cat too. I wanted to bring her but … *(Glancing at her mother.)* I know our neighbors will take care of her till we come back. It'll be great having a cat here. Won't it, Pim? Won't it be fantastic?

MRS. FRANK. Anne dear, don't get so excited. Peter doesn't know you yet.

ANNE. *(Laughing.)* He'll get to know me soon though. It's going to be so much fun having people around. A whole other family. Won't it, Margot?

MARGOT. Yes.

ANNE. *(Skipping around the room.)* Like being on vacation in some strange pension or something. An adventure — romantic and dangerous at the same time!

MR. FRANK. *(Watching Peter's anxious face.)* What is it, Peter?

PETER. My parents. They were right behind me, one street away.

MR. FRANK. *(His hand on Peter's shoulder.)* They'll be here.

PETER. You don't think they were —

MRS. FRANK. Don't worry, Peter. *(She smiles.)* You're just like me.

ANNE. Mother's always jumping at every little thing. *(Peeking into Peter's basket.)* What's its name?

PETER. *(Self-conscious.)* Mouschi.

ANNE. *(To the cat.)* Mouschi! Mouschi. I love cats. *(To Peter.)* Where'd you go to school?

PETER. They set up a technical school in somebody's house, once we were forbidden —

ANNE. *(Breaking in.)* I had to switch from my Montessori school to the Jewish Lyceum.

PETER. I know. I saw you there.

ANNE. You did? *(Mr. Kraler hurries up the stairs with Mr. and Mrs. van Daan. Mrs. van Daan is wearing a fur coat and carrying an umbrella and a large hat box. Mr. van Daan carries a satchel and his briefcase. All three are out of breath.)*

MR. FRANK. *(To Peter, smiling.)* See — what did I tell you? Now we're *all* here.

MR. KRALER. *(Obviously shaken.)* Just in time. We had to take the long way around — there were too many police on the streets. *(Mr. van Daan breaks open a package of cigarettes, nervously starts smoking.)*

MR. FRANK. *(Shaking hands with the van Daans.)* Welcome, Mrs. van Daan. Mr. van Daan. You know my wife, of course, and the children. *(Mrs. Frank, Margot, and Anne shake hands with the van Daans.)*

MR. KRALER. We must hurry. The workmen will be here in half an hour.

MR. FRANK. Such trouble we're causing you, Mr. Kraler, after all you and Miep have done. And now we arrive early!

MR. KRALER. You couldn't let your daughter be taken away, Mr. Frank.

MIEP. Please don't worry. We'll do everything we can to help. Now I must run and get your ration books.

MRS. VAN DAAN. Wait — if they see our names on ration books, won't they know we're here?

MIEP. Trust me — your names won't be on them. If you make a list every day, I'll try to get what you want. And every Saturday I can bring five library books. *(She hurries out.)*

ANNE. Five! I know what my five are going to be.

MRS. FRANK. Anne, remember, there are seven of us.

ANNE. I know, Mother.

MARGOT. *(Troubled.)* It's illegal then, the ration books? We've never done anything illegal.

MR. VAN DAAN. I don't think we'll be living exactly according to regulations here. *(The carillon is heard playing the quarter hour before eight.)*

ANNE. Listen. The Westertoren!

MRS. FRANK. How will I ever get used to that clock?

ANNE. I love it!

MR. KRALER. Miep or I will be here every day to see you. I've hidden a buzzer to signal when we come up, and tomorrow I'll have that bookcase placed in front of your door. Oh, and one last thing ... the radio ... *(He points to a small radio hidden beneath a sheet.)*

ANNE. *(Bounding over to the radio.)* A radio! Fantastic!

MRS. VAN DAAN. A radio. Thank God.

MR. VAN DAAN. How did you get it? We had to turn ours in months ago.

MR. FRANK. Thank you, Mr. Kraler. For everything. *(Mr. Kraler turns to go, as Anne drops a batch of silverware.)*

MR. KRALER. *(To Mr. Frank.)* You'll tell them about the noise?

MR. FRANK. I'll tell them.

MRS. FRANK. *(Following Mr. Kraler to the top of the stairs.)* How can we thank you really? How can we ever —

MR. KRALER. I never thought I'd live to see the day a man like

Mr. Frank would have to go into hiding. *(He hurries out as she stands still, watching him.)*

MR. VAN DAAN. What a journey! It's a wonder we weren't arrested — Petronella walking down the street in a fur coat, carrying a hat box in the middle of summer.

ANNE. What do you need another hat for?

MRS. VAN DAAN. It's not another hat. It's … *(She opens the hat box and pulls out a large chamber pot. Anne and Margot giggle.)*

MRS. FRANK. Oh.

MRS. VAN DAAN. I just don't feel at home without my chamber pot.

MR. FRANK. Now. Everyone. A few things. Quickly! We have to get organized before eight. Anne! Sit down, please. First, about the noise. While the workmen are in the building — from eight to six — we must keep completely quiet. So no shoes. And move only when absolutely necessary. We can't run any water. We can't flush the toilet in the W.C. The pipes go down through the warehouse and every sound can be heard.

MRS. VAN DAAN. Only one toilet? For all of us? *(Mr. Frank nods, as Anne rummages in the carton she is sitting on.)*

MR. FRANK. Anne! No trash can ever be thrown out — not even a potato peel. We'll burn everything in the stove at night. We can't go outside. We can't look out a window. No coughing. If possible, no fevers. Remember — we can never call a doctor. This is the way we must live … until it is over. *(Smiling.)* But … after six we can talk, laugh, play games, move around just as we would at home. This will be our common room, the place we meet to have supper … like one family.

ANNE. One family. I love that!

MR. FRANK. And now why don't we get settled in. As Mr. van Daan and I discussed, this floor will be the van Daan home, the lower floor the Frank home. I know your space is tiny, Peter, but you'll be near your parents. Actually, I'm glad you brought your cat. Miep warns us — there could be rats.

MRS. VAN DAAN. Rats! Oh my God.

MR. VAN DAAN. I'm sure Mouschi can take care of a few rats. Come, Petronella. Let's go up to the attic and bring our dishes down. All our boxes are up there.

MRS. VAN DAAN. *(Shaking Mr. Frank's hand.)* Never, never can we thank you, Mr. Frank. If it weren't for you, I don't know what would have happened to us.

MR. FRANK. You can't imagine how your husband helped me — when I first came to Amsterdam, not knowing a soul, unable to speak the language. I can never repay him. Besides, he's been an excellent business partner.

MR. VAN DAAN. Well, that's true.

MRS. VAN DAAN. *(As they go.)* God, it's hot.

MR. VAN DAAN. If you'd take that precious coat off for one minute, you'd feel a lot cooler. *(He and Mrs. van Daan go up to the attic.)*

MR. FRANK. You rest, Edith. You haven't closed your eyes since yesterday. *(Stroking Margot's cheek.)* Nor you, Margot.

ANNE. I slept, Father. Isn't that funny? Even though I knew it was the last night in my own bed.

MR. FRANK. You. *(Tousling her hair.)* You can sleep through anything. Now take your shoes off, before you forget. You too, Peter. Shoes.

MRS. FRANK. *(Going to their room.)* You're sure you're not too tired, Anneke?

ANNE. Mother. Please. I'm fine. *(Mrs. Frank, Mr. Frank, and Margot make the beds in their rooms. Peter takes a penknife from his pocket, starts to rip off his yellow Star.)* Hey. What are you doing?

PETER. Getting rid of it.

ANNE. *(Moving toward him.)* You can't do that. They'll arrest you if you go out without your star.

PETER. Who's going out? *(He pulls away, goes to the stove.)* Now I don't have to be branded.

ANNE. *(After a moment.)* You're right. We don't need it anymore. *(Trying to rip off her star.)* Remember when it started? People tried to look the other way, but somehow their eyes always landed right there. *(Still struggling.)* Uch, Mother sewed this on so tight.

PETER. The day they made us wear the star was the worst day of my life. *(Lifting the lid of the stove, he throws in the star. Anne pulls at her star, with both hands finally breaks the thread. She stands still, the Star in her hand, then drops it in the stove, closes the lid. On her sweater, the outline of the Star remains.)*

ANNE. Look. It left a mark. *(A step toward him.)* Do you know Hanneli Goslar?

PETER. No.

ANNE. Jopie de Waal?

PETER. Never heard of her.

ANNE. Oh. But you heard of me?

PETER. Well … my father *is* your father's business partner.

ANNE. You heard of me, you heard of me — I'm famous at my school!

PETER. That's true in a way. *(He moves away.)*

ANNE. *(Following him.)* What do you mean?

MR. FRANK. *(Coming in.)* Anne, you mustn't bother Peter.

ANNE. I'm not bothering him. *(Looking into Mouschi's basket.)* Mouschi! Mouschi. Mouschi.

MR. FRANK. Mouschi either. *(Patting Peter's shoulder.)* Tonight we'll have our first real supper here together.

PETER. Thank you. *(He goes into his room.)*

ANNE. He's awfully shy.

MR. FRANK. You'll like him, I know.

ANNE. I better! He's the only boy I'm going to see for — *(Mr. Frank pulls a decorated folder out of a carton. Anne hugs him, grabs the folder.)* My movie stars! Pim, you remembered! I'm going to put them right — wait, where's my diary? *(Rummaging through the carton, she pulls out a hardcover diary, bound in red and white checkered cloth.)* Oh, I forgot to pack my pencils. *(She starts down the stairs.)*

MR. FRANK. *(Quickly moving toward her.)* Anne — no! You can't go down those stairs.

ANNE. *(Slowly coming up.)* But it was only for a —

MR. FRANK. *Never*, Anne! This is what going into hiding means. One mistake could cost us our lives.

ANNE. I know, Father. *(On her bed, Mrs. Frank puts her head in her hands.)*

MR. FRANK. But every day Miep and Mr. Kraler will bring us food, books, their precious company. They're friends, Anne. That's rare these days. If the Nazis found out they were hiding us, they'd be deported too. *(He kisses Anne on the forehead, takes a fountain pen from his breast pocket, holds it out to her.)*

ANNE. Your fountain pen!

MR. FRANK. *Your* fountain pen now.

ANNE. *(Flinging her arms around his neck.)* Oh Pim, Pim! What a darling you are! *(She rushes to her room with the diary and photographs, as the van Daans come down from the attic.)*

MRS. VAN DAAN. All those bags of beans and potatoes — is that what we'll be eating every night? Not much variety, is there? *(Anne puts her diary on the desk, carefully lays the fountain pen beside it.)*

MR. VAN DAAN. *(To Mr. Frank.)* Don't listen to her. What she can do with beans and potatoes … my wife's a great cook.

MR. FRANK. Lucky for us.

MR. VAN DAAN. Even with beans — you'll see. Oh, am I going to miss those gourmet meals!

MRS. VAN DAAN. *(Examining the stove.)* Putti, stop exaggerating.

MR. FRANK. *(Taking Mr. van Daan aside.)* The women seem content, don't they?

MR. VAN DAAN. You can never tell with women. But I think we'll be all right.

MR. FRANK. Good. Mrs. van Daan, we'll meet here at six and start preparing supper.

MRS. VAN DAAN. Six o'clock, yes.

MR. VAN DAAN. Come away from the kitchen, Petronella! The workmen will be here any moment. *(Mr. Frank goes to his room. His wife looks up.)*

MRS. FRANK. Maybe it's a mistake — all of us going into hiding together. They say it's better for families to separate. That way if we're betrayed — caught — at least the children …

MR. FRANK. The children would never have understood if we had separated. They couldn't have borne it. No more than we. *(As the Westertoren chimes eight.)* Come, we must be quiet now. *(The light slowly fades. Margot and Anne sit on Margot's bed.)*

ANNE. Are you all right, Margot?

MARGOT. I'm still shaking. Feel my hands.

ANNE. *(Taking her hands.)* Don't worry. We're here now. They can't take you away.

MARGOT. *(Looking around, overwhelmed.)* Yes. We're here. *(Darkness. In silhouette, Anne and Margot put Anne's movie photo collection up on the wall, as we hear Hitler's deafening voice.)*

HITLER. *(V.O.)* … und für das wir nun einzutreten entschlossen sind, bis zum letzen Hauch, dieses Deutschland der deutschen Volksgemeinschaft aller deutschen Stämme, das grossdeutsche Reich, Sieg Heil! *(As the crowd responds: "Heil!")* Sieg Heil! *(The crowd screams again: "Heil! Heil!" Ferocious applause. Dead silence.)*

ANNE. *(Directly to us.)* It's the silence that frightens me most. Every time I hear a creak in the house, a step on the street, I'm sure they're coming for us. I wander from room to room, feeling like a songbird whose wings have been ripped off and keeps hurling itself against the bars of its cage … Let me out, where there's fresh air and laughter! But then I remember the Jews who are not in hiding, and I know we live in a paradise. We're as quiet as baby mice. Who

17

would have dreamed quicksilver Anne would have to sit still for hours and, what's more, could? *(The light changes. In their room, Mr. Frank sits reading Dickens' David Copperfield, chuckling silently to himself, as Mrs. Frank reads a mystery novel. Margot studies Latin at the desk in her room. Books on the shelves, books on the floor — a real book family. In the main room, Peter tries to study his French. Mrs. van Daan, her fur coat in her lap, sews on a button. Anne lies on the floor, writing in her diary, from time to time cupping her hand over her mouth to stop from laughing. Mrs. van Daan shushes her. In the attic, Mr. van Daan carves a menorah out of wood. Everyone is in their stockinged feet. The sounds of a busy office can be heard below the Annex. The chimes of the Westertoren. Silently, impatiently, Anne moves her legs up and down. Mr. Frank looks at his watch. They are all absolutely still, listening for the door to close behind the last workman. Anne sretches.)* At last! *(Mr. Frank comes up behind Margot, kisses the top of her head, takes her homework from her. Margot takes her shoes, starts toward the W.C.)*

MRS. VAN DAAN. *(Coming up behind Anne.)* What were you writing that was so funny? Nothing about me, I hope. *(Anne slams the diary shut.)* Can't I take a peek?

ANNE. No, Mrs. van Daan.

MRS. VAN DAAN. Not even a little peek?

ANNE. Not even a little peek, Mrs. van Daan. *(She turns away, choking with laughter.)*

MRS. VAN DAAN. All right, fine. I'm first for the W.C.! *(Picking up her shoes, she hurries to the W.C., just as Margot is about to go in. Mrs. van Daan goes ahead. Margot puts on her shoes, begins to help her mother with supper, as Anne hides Peter's shoes behind her back.)*

PETER. Has anyone seen my shoes?

ANNE. *(Innocent.)* Shoes?

PETER. You took them, didn't you?

ANNE. I don't know what you're talking about.

PETER. You're going to be sorry.

ANNE. Am I?

PETER. Definitely. *(He chases her around the table.)*

MRS. FRANK. Anne!

PETER. Wait till I get you!

ANNE. I'm waiting. *(Running around the table.)* I'm waiting, I'm waiting, I'm waiting! *(She stops, holds out his shoes.)* Here. *(Peter wrestles with her to get them away. She struggles delightedly.)* Ooh, you're strong! But you won't get them away from me! *(He tries harder.)* You didn't

18

think I was so strong, did you? *(She laughs wildly.)* Uh-oh, I'm making you mad. You're getting really mad now!

MRS. FRANK. *(Overlapping.)* Anne! Peter! *(Suddenly self-conscious, Peter grabs his shoes, sits down, starts to put them on.)*

ANNE. Come on Peter, dance with me.

PETER. I don't know how.

ANNE. I'll teach you.

PETER. I don't want any lessons.

ANNE. Please.

PETER. I have to give Mouschi his supper.

ANNE. Can I watch?

PETER. He doesn't like people around when he eats.

ANNE. I'll be quiet. Quiet as a little mouse. He likes mice, doesn't he?

PETER. No! *(Pushing her out, he slams the door of his room.)*

MRS. FRANK. You shouldn't play with Peter like that. It's not dignified.

ANNE. *(Putting on her shoes.)* I don't want to be dignified.

MRS. FRANK. You complain I don't treat you like a grownup, but when I do, you resent it.

ANNE. I just want to have some fun. What's wrong with that boy?

MR. FRANK. He's not used to girls. Especially a girl like our Anneke. Give him time.

ANNE. How much time does he need? *(Catching hold of Margot.)* You dance with me, Margot!

MARGOT. I have to help with supper.

ANNE. C'mon! If we don't practice, we'll forget. *(Humming, she begins to waltz Margot around the room.)*

MARGOT. *(Laughing.)* All right, all right. *(She waltzes with Anne. She is a wonderful dancer.)*

ANNE. See, everyone? Margot's the real dancer in the family. *(Margot whirls her around, right into the arms of Mr. Frank.)* Pim! *(They do a few turns together. She squeals happily as he lifts her in the air.)*

MRS. VAN DAAN. *(Coming back into the room.)* Ah, dancing. Where's Peter?

MARGOT. In his room.

MRS. VAN DAAN. His father'll kill him if he catches him with that cat again. Anne darling, do me a favor and get Peter out of his room. *(Humming a different waltz, she moves toward Mr. Frank, swaying back and forth. Reluctantly, Anne goes toward Peter's room, as*

Mrs. van Daan opens her arms, inviting Mr. Frank to dance. Hesitant at first, he begins waltzing with her.)

ANNE. *(Knocking on Peter's door, as she watches Mrs. van Daan dance with her father.)* Peter? Oh, Peter.

PETER. *(Opening the door a crack.)* What is it?

ANNE. Your mother says to come out.

MRS. VAN DAAN. You know what your father says.

ANNE. I'll feed Mouschi.

PETER. All right. But just give him his supper and come right out. *(He comes into the main room, as Anne shuts the door of his room behind her.)*

MRS. VAN DAAN. Is that any way to talk to your little girlfriend?

PETER. Mother! Please.

MRS. VAN DAAN. Look — he's blushing!

PETER. You're crazy. She's only thirteen.

MRS. VAN DAAN. So? You're sixteen. Your father's older than I am. I tell you, Mr. Frank, if this war lasts much longer we're liable to be related. *(Humming again, she hitches up her skirt, checks her stocking.)* Oh, I think I have a run here. *(Peter rolls his eyes.)*

PETER. Some run. *(The sudden sound of a siren approaching. Everyone freezes. A squad car comes closer, its siren blaring. It passes them, continues on.)*

MRS. VAN DAAN. *(Shaken.)* God, I hate them. *(Anne opens the door of Peter's room, dressed in his heavy coat and cap. Peter stares at her.)*

ANNE. *(Moving awkwardly.)* Good evening, everyone. I wish I could stay for supper, but I'm so shy I can barely get a word out of my —

PETER. *(Wheeling on her, opening and closing his hand before his mouth.)* All right! I heard about you. How you talked so much in class Mr. Keesing called you Miss Quack Quack, and made you write a composition — "'Quack, quack, quack,' said Miss Quack Quack."

ANNE. Well, go on! Tell them the rest. How it was so good he read it out loud to our class and all his other classes!

PETER. I know about you — always joking.

ANNE. I don't always joke.

PETER. Always making fun of — mocking people — "Quack, quack, quack!"

ANNE. I don't always — *(Throwing his cap at him.)* You're the most infuriating boy I've ever met! *(She tears off the coat, throws it at him too.)*

MRS. VAN DAAN. That's right, Anne. You give it to him.

ANNE. With all the boys in the world, I had to get locked up with —

PETER. *(Grabbing his clothes.)* Quack, quack, quack — and from now on stay out of my room! *(As he starts toward his room, Anne puts out her foot, tripping him. He picks himself up, stares at her, seething, as Anne laughs.)*

MRS. FRANK. Anne.

MR. FRANK. *(Looking up from correcting papers.)* Excellent in History, Anne! And in Latin.

MR. VAN DAAN. *(Coming down from the attic.)* Miep's not here yet?

MRS. VAN DAAN. The workmen only left a little while ago.

MR. VAN DAAN. What's for dinner?

MRS. VAN DAAN. *(Sorting through a bowl of dried beans.)* Beans.

MR. VAN DAAN. Again? *(Turning to Peter.)* I saw you in there, playing with that cat.

MRS. VAN DAAN. He just went in for a second. He's been out here all afternoon working on his French.

MR. VAN DAAN. Really.

ANNE. *(To her father.)* How did I do in Algebra?

MR. FRANK. *(Grinning.)* I think we *both* better give up on Algebra.

MARGOT. How did I do?

ANNE. How do you always do? *(Patting her head.)* Brilliant!

MR. FRANK. You might have used the subjunctive here.

MARGOT. Where? *(She and her father become absorbed in her work. Anne turns away, stares at Mrs. van Daan's coat.)*

ANNE. Mrs. van Daan. May I try on your coat?

MRS. FRANK. Anne.

MRS. VAN DAAN. *(Holding up the coat for Anne to slip into.)* Of course you may. My father gave me this coat the year before he died. He always bought the best money could buy. *(A glance at her husband.)*

ANNE. Did you have a lot of boyfriends before you were married?

MRS. FRANK. Anne, it's not courteous to ask personal questions.

ANNE. Why not? I had a throng of admirers who couldn't keep their eyes off me.

MRS. VAN DAAN. Our house was always swarming with boys. I remember the summer I was sixteen —

MR. VAN DAAN. *(Tossing cards into a large pot on the floor.)* Oh, God. Here we go again!

MRS. VAN DAAN. Who's talking to you? *(Anne listens, fascinated, following her, imitating her walk.)* We had a big house in Bremer-haven. Those boys came buzzing like bees around a honey-pot. *(Mr. van Daan chuckles.)* My father was very worried with all those

21

boys buzzing around. He'd say, "If any of them gets fresh, you tell him … 'Remember, Mr. So-and-So, remember I'm a lady.'"

ANNE. *(Imitating her.)* "Remember, Mr. So-and-So, remember I'm a lady."

MRS. VAN DAAN. *(Laughing, hugging her.)* Very good. *(She takes her coat back.)* All right, that's enough. *(She lays the coat carefully on the couch as Anne quickly picks up her diary, sprawls on the floor, writing.)*

MR. VAN DAAN. What have you got to write about that's so important all the time? How much does a thirteen-year-old have to say?

MARGOT. Just because someone's young doesn't mean they don't have anything to say, Mr. van Daan.

ANNE. Please. Can't I have any privacy?

MR. VAN DAAN. Petronella, can you please tell me what could possibly be so private.

MRS. VAN DAAN. Oh, you know how it is at that age, Putti. Everything's private. Even brushing your teeth.

MR. VAN DAAN. I just hope she doesn't write anything about *me* in that private diary of hers.

MRS. VAN DAAN. *(Laughing.)* Don't be ridiculous! Really, Putti, you're so childish sometimes. *(Anne stifles a laugh.)*

MR. VAN DAAN. *(To Peter.)* Still haven't finished your French? You ought to be ashamed.

PETER. I know, I know. I'm a hopeless case.

MRS. VAN DAAN. You are not hopeless. *(To her husband.)* He is not hopeless. He just doesn't have anyone to help him, like the girls do. Maybe you could, Mr. Frank.

MR. FRANK. I'm sure his father —

MR. VAN DAAN. Not me. He won't listen to me.

MR. FRANK. What do you say, Peter?

MRS. VAN DAAN. Oh Mr. Frank, you're an angel! *(Kissing the top of his head.)* I don't know why I didn't meet you before I met that one over there.

MR. FRANK. *(Uncomfortable.)* Come, Peter. Show me which chapter you're on.

MRS. VAN DAAN. *(As Peter and Mr. Frank go into Peter's room.)* You listen to Mr. Frank, Peter. Mr. Frank is a highly educated man. *(Mr. van Daan nearly trips over Anne, who lies on her stomach, writing.)*

MR. VAN DAAN. *(Stepping over her.)* Aren't things hard enough without you sprawling all over the place?

22

MRS. VAN DAAN. If you didn't smoke so much, Putti, you wouldn't be so ill-tempered.

MR. VAN DAAN. Am I smoking? Do you see me smoking?

MRS. VAN DAAN. Don't tell me you used up all those cigarettes.

MR. VAN DAAN. One package! Miep only brought one package.

MRS. VAN DAAN. You're smoking up all our money.

MR. VAN DAAN. Will you shut up? *(Mrs. Frank and Margot keep their eyes down as Anne, sitting on the floor, follows the whole exchange. Seeing her staring up at him.)* What are you staring at?

ANNE. I never heard grownups quarrel before. I thought only children quarreled and it wore off when you grew up.

MR. VAN DAAN. This isn't a quarrel — it's a discussion. And I never heard children so rude before.

ANNE. *(Jumping to her feet.)* Rude, me? I don't know how *you* can say that when —

MRS. FRANK. Anne dear, would you please bring me my knitting. I must remember to ask Miep for more wool.

MARGOT. I have a library book for her to return. And I need some hairpins and soap.

ANNE. *(Giving her mother the wool.)* Please Miep, get me some starch. Some tea, some biscuits, a movie star magazine. Tell us all the latest news, Miep. Miep, Miep, Miep! It's a wonder Miep has a life of her own! Did you know she's engaged to someone called Jan? She's crazy about him, but terrified the Nazis will send him to Germany to work in a war plant. That's what they do with all the young Dutchmen these days. They pick them up in the street and —

MR. VAN DAAN. *(Slamming down the lid of a trunk.)* Suppose you try keeping still for five minutes! *(Anne clamps her lips tight.)*

MRS. FRANK. Anne, come have your milk.

MR. VAN DAAN. Talk, talk, talk! Chatter, chatter, chatter. It's a wonder we haven't been discovered and shot. Why do you have to show off all the time? Can't you be quiet like your sister Margot? Be a good girl.

ANNE. Not me! *(Dancing past him with the milk.)* I'm going to be remarkable. I'm going to Paris.

MR. VAN DAAN. Really.

ANNE. You'll see. I'm going to be a famous writer or singer or dancer one day! *(Twirling, glass in hand, she spills the milk over Mrs. van Daan's fur coat, hastily tries to brush it away.)*

MRS. VAN DAAN. *(Rushing toward the coat.)* Oh my God! My coat. My beautiful fur coat!

ANNE. I'm sorry.

MRS. VAN DAAN. Do you know what my father paid for this coat? Look at it!

ANNE. I'm very very sorry.

MRS. VAN DAAN. I could kill you for this.

MR. VAN DAAN. Petronella! *(He helps her clean the coat.)*

MRS. FRANK. *(Pulling Anne into her room, Margot behind them.)* Anne, you can't behave like this.

ANNE. It was an accident. Anyone can have an accident.

MRS. FRANK. I'm not just talking about the coat, Anne. We're all living under great stress, but you don't hear Margot getting into arguments with the van Daans, do you?

ANNE. Margot's perfect. She never gets into arguments with anyone.

MARGOT. I'm not perfect.

MRS. FRANK. She's courteous. She keeps her distance and they respect her for it. Try to be more like Margot.

ANNE. And have them walk over me too? No thank you.

MARGOT. They don't walk over me!

ANNE. Oh yes they do. *All* over you.

MRS. FRANK. I'm not afraid they'll walk over you, Anne. I'm afraid you'll walk over them. I don't know what happens to you. If I ever talked to my mother the way you talk to me —

ANNE. "Yes Mother, no Mother, anything you say Mother." People aren't like that anymore. I can't do everything for you.

MRS. FRANK. Margot doesn't do everything —

ANNE. Margot, Margot! That's all I ever hear.

MARGOT. Anne, don't be so dramatic!

ANNE. Everything she does is right, and everything I do is wrong. If I talk, I'm a show-off, if I answer, I'm rude, selfish if I eat too much, stupid, cowardly, a complete disappointment! I'll never live up to your expectations. I'll never be Margot! *(Sobbing, she runs into her parents room.)*

MRS. FRANK. I don't know how we can go on living like this.

MARGOT. You know Anne. In two minutes she'll be laughing and joking again.

MRS. FRANK. No room, no privacy — for any of us. *(Gesturing toward the van Daans.)* Uch … those people! The way they behave. And your father chooses to shut his eyes to these things. *(Margot*

24

reaches toward her.) I can't even remember how life used to be. *(The shrill sound of the buzzer.)*

MARGOT and MRS. FRANK. Miep! *(They grab their lists and hurry to the main room, as Mr. Frank and Peter come out of Peter's room.)*

PETER. It's Miep.

MRS. VAN DAAN. Miep! Our darling Miep!

MR. VAN DAAN. At last.

MR. FRANK. Does everyone have their list?

MRS. VAN DAAN. I have mine. *(All seven of them line up, lists in hand, as Miep appears, her arms full of groceries.)*

MRS. FRANK. *(Going to Anne.)* Now you'll get your library book, darling. *(Anne pulls away, runs to Miep, sniffing her clothes, her face.)*

ANNE. Oh, Miep, Miep — that air! What's it like … outside? *(Mr. Kraler appears behind Miep.)*

MR. FRANK. How are you, Mr. Kraler?

ANNE. *(To Miep.)* Where did you go today? Who did you see? Did anyone interesting come into the office?

MR. VAN DAAN. *(Opening a fresh pack of cigarettes.)* When Miep comes the sun begins to shine!

MARGOT. We missed you yesterday, Mr. Kraler.

ANNE. Tell us, Miep. We want to know everything.

MRS. FRANK. Won't you stay for supper?

MIEP. Thank you, but there's something we need to talk over. Something that has to be decided immediately.

MRS. VAN DAAN. What? What is it, Mr. Kraler?

MR. KRALER. Each time we come, we try and bring a bit of good news. But up here you just can't know how bad things have become outside. *(He looks at Miep.)*

MIEP. There's a dentist — Alfred Dussel. He's Jewish. He's been living with a Christian woman, but today he asked if I knew of a safe address. He's desperate. *(Quiet.)* I promised I would let him know. *(Silence.)*

MR. FRANK. *(Stepping forward.)* Of course, Miep. Absolutely. Dussel. I believe we know him.

ANNE. It's great news, Miep!

MR. VAN DAAN. Yes. But where is he going to sleep? There's barely enough room …

MR. FRANK. Forgive me. I spoke without consulting you. I was sure —

MR. VAN DAAN. It's just that … there's so little food.

25

MIEP. Mr. van Daan, I've tried. There are no more ration books to be had.

MR. FRANK. Where seven can eat, eight can eat as well.

MR. VAN DAAN. I hope so.

MR. FRANK. If we can save even one person we must.

MR. VAN DAAN. *(Shaking his hand.)* Well, you're right. Of course.

MRS. VAN DAAN. *(As the others agree.)* Yes. Definitely.

MIEP. Mr. Kraler will go to meet him. I will bring him up.

MR. KRALER. Tomorrow! *(He leaves, Miep behind him, collecting lists and library books.)*

MIEP. *(Turning back. A grave smile.)* Thank you. *(She leaves.)*

MRS. VAN DAAN. It's fine to have him, but where are we going to put him?

PETER. He can have my bed. I'll sleep on the floor.

MR. FRANK. You're very kind, Peter. But there's hardly enough room in there for you.

ANNE. I know! I'll move in with you and Mother, and Mr. Dussel can have my bed.

MRS. FRANK. No. No, no. Margot will move in with us, and Mr. Dussel can have her bed. It's the only way.

ANNE. But why? Why can't *I* move in?

MRS. FRANK. Because it wouldn't be proper for Margot to — Please, Anne, don't argue. It's settled. *(Anne stands up, bangs down her chair, rushes into her room, slams the door behind her. She grabs her diary, sits at the desk, starts writing feverishly.)*

ANNE. *(Directly to us.)* As far as I'm concerned Mother can go jump in a lake! I don't know why I've taken such a terrible dislike to her, but I can imagine her dying someday, while Papa's death seems inconceivable to me. It's very mean of me I know, but that's how I feel. I hope Mother will never read this or anything else I've written. She's not a mother to me — I have to mother myself. Who can I turn to? Only my diary. I have to become a good person on my own, but I know it will make me stronger in the end. *(Anne gets up from her desk as the others prepare for the new arrival.)* Three and a half months in the Annex and we're eagerly awaiting our latest addition. What will he be like? Miep says he's quiet, refined *and*, by all accounts, an excellent dentist! *(A delighted low laugh. Mr. Frank, reading his Dickens, chuckles at the edge of the stage. As Mrs. Frank urges him to get ready, the light opens up to reveal the other residents standing at the head of the stairs. A bottle of cognac and six glasses are set out on the table.)* He's meeting Mr. Kraler at eleven sharp this morning at a certain place in front of the post office. It's all very exciting … and totally nerve-racking. What if they get caught? Those last hours are the most dangerous for a Jew who goes into hiding. *(Miep leads Mr. Dussel up the stairs. He stops, stunned, as the seven smile, hold out their hands.)*

MIEP. *(A great smile.)* Ladies and gentlemen. It's done. *(She helps Mr. Dussel take off an ill-fitting coat. Underneath is his white office jacket with the yellow star.)*

ANNE. *(Directly to us, as Mr. Dussel shakes everyone's hand.)* Every-thing went smoothly. Mr. Dussel was at the appointed place at the appointed time. He had to wear Jan's coat over his office jacket, so no one would see the yellow star. He was amazed to be brought to the center of Amsterdam rather than into the country, where so many hiding places are. Of course he had no idea we were right upstairs, waiting for him!

MR. DUSSEL. *(As Mr. Frank holds out his hand.)* I'm dreaming. Mr. Frank? Otto Frank? I heard you were in Switzerland. A patient of mine told me you'd escaped to Basel. Or Belgium. Or some-place! *(Everyone laughs.)*

MR. FRANK. That's what everyone thinks. The Nazis included, we hope.

ANNE. We tricked them!

MARGOT. We're so glad you've come, Mr. Dussel.

MRS. VAN DAAN. We all are.

MR. DUSSEL. How can I thank you?

MR. VAN DAAN. Not us. Miep and Mr. Kraler.

MRS. FRANK. Without them we couldn't live.

ANNE. Aren't you scared, Miep? Sometimes?

MIEP. We're not heroes.

MR. FRANK. You're much too modest, Miep.

MIEP. We just don't like the Nazis. Anything about them.

MR. FRANK. Come, Mr. Dussel. Sit down. You must be worn out.

MR. VAN DAAN. Let's all have a little toast to Mr. Dussel.

MRS. VAN DAAN. Cognac! We were saving it in case of illness, but —

MR. FRANK. What better way to use it? *(Lifting his glass.)* To Mr. Dussel. We're honored to have you with us.

MR. VAN DAAN. Prost.

EVERYONE. Prost! *(All but Anne and Margot lift their glasses to Mr. Dussel, who quietly gulps down his cognac.)*

MRS. VAN DAAN. Mmmm. Delicious. Too bad there's so little of it.

MR. FRANK. I believe we know someone in common, Mr. Dussel.

MR. DUSSEL. Ah?

MR. FRANK. Dr. Kinzler. We were friends back in the old days in Frankfort — *(Mr. Dussel goes white.)* What? What is it?

MR. DUSSEL. Dr. Kinzler was taken last month. Beethovenstraat. They took the whole block. *(Mrs. Frank gasps.)*

MRS. VAN DAAN. Mr. Dussel. What is happening outside?

MRS. FRANK. Tell us. *(Anne moves closer, sits on the floor before Mr. Dussel.)*

MR. DUSSEL. All over Amsterdam, Jews are disappearing … torn out of bed in the middle of the night … My God, the screams. Children come home from school — their parents are gone. Women come back from shopping — whole families … vanished. It's impossible to escape unless you go into hiding. Thousands are being taken away. Deported. The Blumbergs, Professor Hallenstein —

MRS. VAN DAAN. *(Falling back.)* Oh God, no.

MR. DUSSEL. You have five minutes to get ready. Bring only what you can carry in a rucksack. Herded into the Jewish Theatre for days, weeks sometimes, and then … Westerbork. The transit camp. From there, every Tuesday, like clockwork, a train leaves for … the East. *(A moment of stunned silence.)*

ANNE. Mr. Dussel, do you know the Goslars? Their daughter Hanneli and I — we've been friends since we were four. They … they didn't come for them, did they? *(Mr. Dussel looks at Mr. Frank, then back at Anne, silent. She leaps up.)* Not Hanneli! It can't be! *(In tears she moves away, Margot following, comforting her.)*

PETER. There's a family by the name of —

MRS. FRANK. *(A sudden cry.)* No!

MR. FRANK. I'm sure Mr. Dussel needs to get settled before supper. *(To Mr. Dussel.)* I'm sorry we can't offer you your own room. I trust you won't mind sharing one with my daughter.

MR. DUSSEL. Forgive me for upsetting you.

MRS. FRANK. No. You had to tell us. We had to know.

MR. FRANK. Anne, why don't you show Mr. Dussel your room?

MR. DUSSEL. *(As Miep starts to leave.)* Miep. Thank you for everything.

MARGOT. All he said … so terrible, so different from what Mr. Kraler's been telling us.

MR. VAN DAAN. *(Quiet.)* I like it better the way Kraler tells it. *(Mrs. Frank follows Miep down a few steps. At the bottom step, Miep looks up. Silent, Mrs. Frank stares down at her.)*

ANNE. *(Coming into her room with Mr. Dussel.)* Well, here we are.

MR. DUSSEL. Ah. *(Looking around.)* It isn't very big, is it?

ANNE. I've never shared a room with a man before. I hope I'll be a suitable companion. *(He stares at her, taken aback.)* I know you'll miss the woman you live with terribly.

MR. DUSSEL. Charlotte and I have never been apart. It all happened so quickly, I couldn't tell her where I was going. I didn't know myself.

ANNE. You weren't supposed to. None of our friends knew — it would have been too dangerous. Not just for us. For them and ... for Charlotte.

MR. DUSSEL. You're a very bright young lady. I hope you'll bear with me.

ANNE. I hope you'll bear with *me*! *(Cheerfully.)* I seem to irritate everyone around here. *(Coming closer.)* What's she like ... your Charlotte?

MR. DUSSEL. Charming. Beautiful. You would like her. *(A moment.)* She's not Jewish, you know.

ANNE. *(In a rush.)* Oh I know. Miep told us. That's my bed. And that's Margot's, where you'll sleep. I know it's small and dark in here, but if you peek through the blackout curtain you'll see the most beautiful chestnut tree in the world. I can't wait till it's in blossom, though I hope the war will be over by then and we'll all be home. *(He backs away. She pauses.)* I was wondering ... about the room ... Margot always had it in the afternoons and I had it in the mornings. Would that be all right with you?

MR. DUSSEL. Actually, I'm not at my best in the morning.

ANNE. Then you take the mornings, and I'll take the afternoons. Did you bring your dental equipment? *(She reaches for his little black bag, which he instantly picks up.)* I can't wait to see it! I love those little mirrors. Will you fill all our cavities?

MR. DUSSEL. It's very hard being a dentist, you know. Children don't understand that.

ANNE. What do you mean?

MR. DUSSEL. No one likes going to the dentist. Everyone makes fun of dentists but, believe me, it's no fun for us. Everyone hates us.

ANNE. That's awful.

MR. DUSSEL. Tell me something. When you're in here, where do I go? In there, with all those people?

ANNE. *(Sitting down on Mr. Dussel's bed.)* And Mouschi.

MR. DUSSEL. Who's Mouschi?

ANNE. *(Laughing.)* Peter's cat.

MR. DUSSEL. Cat! No one mentioned a cat to me. He has it here?

ANNE. Oh you'll love Mouschi. He's the sweetest cat in the world.

MR. DUSSEL. I hate cats! They're terrifying. They give me asthma.

ANNE. Don't worry. Peter keeps him in his room all the time.

MR. DUSSEL. Let us hope so. *(Anne, taken aback, looks away.)* By the way, Mr. Kraler spoke of a schedule.

ANNE. It's mainly about when we have to be quiet, and when we can use the W.C. You can use it now if you —

MR. DUSSEL. No. Thank you.

ANNE. You don't know how important the W.C. can be when you're in hiding … especially when you're scared.

MR. DUSSEL. I understand. *(Silence.)* If you don't mind, I think I'll lie down before supper. It helps with the digestion. *(Quickly Anne gets up off his bed, squeezes past him in the small space.)*

ANNE. You rest, Mr. Dussel. I'll try and make you feel at home. *(She touches him lightly. He jumps, taken off-guard, then tentatively takes her hand … Darkness, as Anne gets ready for bed. A broadcast begins.)*

BROADCAST. *(V.O.)* This is Colin Reese Parker with the BBC Radio Europe, November twelfth. Yesterday German forces entered unoccupied France. Acting quickly to counter sweeping Allied gains, Hitler sent armored columns to occupy Vichy, France. The Vichy Regime came to an end, and with it, the final pretense that part of France was a "Free Zone."

ANNE. *(From her bed.)* I couldn't sleep tonight, even after Father tucked me in. I feel wicked sleeping in a warm bed when my friends are at the mercy of the cruelest monsters ever to walk the earth. And all because they're Jews. We assume most of them are murdered. The BBC says they're being gassed. Perhaps that's the quickest way to die. *(As she continues, Mr. van Daan, at the table, tries vainly to light a cigarette butt, burns his finger.)* No matter what I'm doing, I can't stop thinking about those who are gone. All we can do is wait for the war to end. The whole world is waiting, and many are waiting for death. *(She lies down, goes to sleep as, from a distance, marching feet approach. Close, closer. From the street, the Nazi "Horst Wessel-Song" builds to a crescendo. Voiceover, a Barrack Head of Westerbork breaks in.)*

BARRACK HEAD. *(V.O.)* Achtung! Achtung! The list for Tuesday's train! One thousand will leave Westerbork tomorrow for labor service in the East! No exemptions! *(The cattle-car door slides shut. The shattering sound of a train whistle.)*

ANNE. *(Screaming in her sleep.)* No! No! Don't let them take me!

MR. DUSSEL. For God's sake, be quiet!

ANNE. I won't! I won't get on the train!

MR. DUSSEL. *(Bending over her.)* Shhh! You'll get us all killed! *(Mrs. Frank rushes in, takes Anne in her arms.)*

MRS. FRANK. Anne, darling. You're here. Safe. *(As Anne comes out of her nightmare.)* It was a dream, my angel. You were having a dream.

MR. DUSSEL. These nightmares, Mrs. Frank, they're getting worse. I don't sleep anymore. I spend half my night shushing her.

MRS. FRANK. Anne. Little Anne.

MR. DUSSEL. Every night, Mrs. Frank, every night. She's putting us all in danger.

MRS. FRANK. Please, Mr. Dussel, go back to bed. She'll be all right in a minute. *(Mr. Dussel leaves.)*

PETER. *(Coming out of his room.)* What happened?

MR. DUSSEL. Another nightmare.

MR. VAN DAAN. It sounded like someone was murdering her. *(Mr. Dussel raises his eyebrows, goes into the W.C.)*

MRS. FRANK. Can I get you some water? *(As Anne shakes her head.)* It was a bad dream, wasn't it? Do you want to tell me? Sometimes it helps —

ANNE. No. Thank you, Mother.

MRS. FRANK. Try to sleep now. I'll sit right beside you till —

ANNE. I'd rather you didn't. *(Silence.)*

MRS. FRANK. I see. Good night then. *(She leans down to kiss her. Anne turns away.)*

ANNE. *(In tears, her voice muffled, hesitant.)* Would you ask Father to come in? *(Hurt, Mrs. Frank stands still.)* Please. *(Mrs. Frank hurries out as Mr. Frank is on his way in.)*

MR. FRANK. Edith.

MRS. FRANK. She wants you, Otto. She's still trembling. *(He hesitates.)* It's all right. Go to her. *(He leaves. Margot puts her arms around her mother.)*

MARGOT. It's a phase.

MRS. FRANK. You weren't like this.

MARGOT. I'm more like you. It's not that she doesn't love you. *(Mr. Frank goes into Anne's room.)*

ANNE. *(Flinging her arms around him.)* Oh Pim, Pim! I dreamt they broke through the bookcase, took us all away. The train whistle, Pim! The train going to the East! *(He is silent.)* Did I yell terribly loud? Do you think anyone heard outside? *(He remains still.)* I know what you're thinking. But I can't help the way I feel. I just don't love her!

MR. FRANK. Anne!

ANNE. We don't get along. We never have. And now — I hate being cooped up with her! I don't get along with anyone here. My nightmares, Pim! Everyone hates me for having them. I can't stop them from coming.

MR. FRANK. We're all having nightmares, Anne. Only you let them out. Your mother has them too. Terrible nightmares. She's having a very hard time.

ANNE. I know. I know, Pim. I'm trying to change. I have another side, a better finer side. But it's as if I'm split in half. What's good, what's bad, Pim? I don't know. I want to be a better person, but not if it means shutting myself off. Hiding how I feel.

MR. FRANK. I understand. We've always understood each other — you and I. *(A pause.)* You know, Anneke, you taught me something the day we came here.

ANNE. Me?

MR. FRANK. Remember when we arrived — your mother and Margot were numb. Couldn't speak. Couldn't move. I was a wreck with worry, but you ... you skipped around the room calling it "an adventure." You showed me you could escape. Now, when I read my Dickens, it takes me to another world. In that world I feel safe. *(A pause.)* You have something too. A diary. You're lucky.

ANNE. Lucky?

MR. FRANK. You can write. You can put all your thoughts, all your feelings, down on paper ... *(The fierce sound of planes overhead. The sound of an air raid siren. Bombs falling. A burst of machine-gun fire. Darkness. Anne clings to her father. The van Daans rush toward Peter. Mrs. Frank and Margot hold each other close.)*

ANNE. The house is shaking!

MR. FRANK. It's all right, Anne. The more planes, the sooner the war will end. *(The sound of the air raid siren blends into voices praying quietly in Hebrew, as light comes up on Mr. Dussel in the attic, wearing a prayer shawl, swaying back and forth. The voices continue as he prays softly.)*

MR. DUSSEL. *(In Hebrew.)*
> Sim shalom tova u'vrachah
> Chain vo'chesed v'rachamim
> Olainu v'al kol yisroel amechoh.

(Light comes up on Anne at her desk, writing. She looks up, speaks directly to us.)

ANNE. Tonight, after the radio broadcast, Pim asked what was the first thing we wanted to do when we're liberated. I'd be so thrilled I wouldn't know where to begin. I long to be back in school with my friends, ride a bike, whistle, laugh so hard it hurts. I wonder if anyone will ever not think about whether I'm Jewish — just a young girl badly in need of some good plain fun. Margot said ...

MARGOT. I want to go dancing! Learn the latest step and fly all over the room in a new pair of dancing shoes.

PETER. The movies! I'd love to go to a movie. A Western! If they ever decide to let us in again.

MRS. FRANK. I'm longing for a real cup of coffee ... with cream. And sugar. No — a whole potful!

MRS. VAN DAAN. A bath. A hot bath ... in a bathtub. Lying there luxuriating for hours, and then Putti comes in and soaps my back.

ANNE. And Putti said ...

MR. VAN DAAN. Cream cakes! First thing out of here, I'm going to Berkhof's for cream cakes.

MR. DUSSEL. Charlotte. Just to look at her. Listen to her. For hours.

MR. FRANK. You know what I want? To pack a picnic lunch and take my family to the seashore ... for the whole day. *(... Hanukkah. The first night. December 1942. Standing around the kitchen table, they admire the wooden menorah Mr. van Daan has made.)*

MARGOT. What a beautiful menorah, Mr. van Daan! *(Peter lights the two candles.)*

THE WOMEN. *(In Hebrew.)*
> Ba-ruch a-ta A-do-nai
> E-lo-hei-nu me-lech ha-o-lam
> a-sher ki-de-sha-nu be-mits-vo-tav
> ve-tsi-va-nu le-had-lik neir
> shel Cha-nu-ka.

EVERYONE. Amen.

MR. DUSSEL. *(Taking off his yarmulke.)* That was very moving.

ANNE. It's not over yet. There's still the song. Presents!

MR. VAN DAAN. *(As Anne rushes out.)* Not this year.

MRS. VAN DAAN. And no latkes either.

MR. VAN DAAN. Don't remind me!

MRS. VAN DAAN. I make the best latkes you ever tasted.

MR. VAN DAAN. Please. I can't bear it.

MR. FRANK. Invite us all next year. *(Anne rushes back, clutching her bulging schoolbag.)*

MRS. FRANK. What's in there, darling?

ANNE. Presents! *(She pulls out a manila envelope.)* For Margot — read it out loud.

MARGOT. *(Reading a poem on the envelope.)*
"You never lose your temper,
    You never will, I fear
    You're just so good
    But if you should,
    Put all your cross words here."

(She takes out a thin book.) A new crossword puzzle book!

ANNE. It's not new — it's yours — I rubbed it all out, but if you wait a while and forget, you can do it all over again!

MARGOT. *(Embracing her.)* Oh Anne, it's wonderful!

ANNE. For Mrs. van Daan.

MRS. VAN DAAN. *(Taking a slender bottle of green liquid from a scrap of paper.)* How beautiful! What's in it?

ANNE. Shampoo. I took all the tiny pieces of soap and mixed them with the last of my toilet water.

MRS. VAN DAAN. *(Hugging her.)* How sweet! Thank you, Anne.

MR. FRANK. This was all Anne's idea.

ANNE. For Mr. van Daan. This is *really* something … something you want more than anything in the world.

MR. VAN DAAN. Oh my goodness — I can't wait. What can it be? *(Opening a small box.)* A cigarette.

ANNE. Pim found some old pipe tobacco in the pocket lining of his coat, and we made it … well, Pim did. But it's real tobacco. I promise.

MR. VAN DAAN. We'll see. *(Everyone watches as Mrs. Frank lights the cigarette for Mr. van Daan, who inhales deeply several times, chokes. Hoarsely.)* Thank you, Anne. *(Everyone laughs.)* I mean it. Truly.

ANNE. *(Handing her mother a piece of paper.)* For Mother.

MRS. FRANK. *(Reading.)*
"Here's an I.O.U. I promise to pay.
    Ten hours of doing whatever you say."

(Touched, she holds Anne close.)

MR. DUSSEL. Boy, I wish I had that little slip of paper. Ten hours! You wouldn't consider selling it, would you, Mrs. Frank?

MRS. FRANK. Never! It's the best present I've ever had. *(She shows it around, as Anne pulls out another present, shyly gives it to her father.)*

ANNE. For Pim.

MR. FRANK. Anne, I'm not supposed to get anything. *(He undoes the wrapping. A crudely knit scarf, narrow in the center, huge on the ends, falls out.)* Oh!

ANNE. I made it out of bits of wool I found. No one helped me. Not even Mother. Not even Margot. I knitted it in the dark after I got into bed.

MR. DUSSEL. And after keeping me up half the night — writing in that diary of hers! *(Grinning.)* Just kidding.

ANNE. I'm afraid it looks better in the dark.

MR. FRANK. It looks perfect to me. *(He puts it on, hugs his daughter.)* Thank you, Anneke. I shall treasure it. *(Anne hands Peter a small ball of yarn with ribbons attached.)*

ANNE. For Mouschi.

MARGOT. Oh Anne — the ribbons from your ballet shoes.

PETER. On behalf of Mouschi, thank you. It's very sweet of you.

ANNE. *(Handing him a little case.)* And ... from Miss Quack Quack. Go ahead. Open it.

PETER. You're sure nothing's going to jump out and bite me?

MRS. VAN DAAN. *(As he opens the present.)* What is it?

ANNE. *(Unable to contain her excitement.)* A razor! Miep got it for me. And you really do need one now.

MR. DUSSEL. What for?

ANNE. Look at his upper lip. There's a little something growing there.

MR. DUSSEL. There is? Well, put a little milk on it and let the cat lick it off. *(He laughs wildly, the others silent, as Peter stands up, glares at him.)*

PETER. Think you're funny, do you? Well, I like it. Thanks, Anne. *(He goes into his room.)*

ANNE. *(Tossing the last present on the table.)* And last but never least, my roommate, Mr. Dussel.

MR. DUSSEL. You got something for me, Anne. *(He opens the tiny box.)* Capsules. Two capsules. *(A pause.)* Not poison, I hope.

ANNE. Earplugs! So you won't hear me thrashing around at night. I made them out of cotton and candle wax. Go ahead, try them. See if they work. *(Mr. Dussel puts them in his ears.)* Ready?

MR. DUSSEL. What?

ANNE. *(Louder.)* Are you ready?

MR. DUSSEL. *(An agonized look on his face.)* Good God, they've gone inside my head! Help! Help! *(He thumps his head frantically, finally removes them, holds out his hand to Anne.)* I was joking. Thank you, Anne.

MARGOT. *(Overlapping.)* I love my present!

MRS. FRANK. *(Overlapping.)* I don't know how she did it.

MRS. VAN DAAN. *(Overlapping.)* Wasn't it darling of her?

MR. VAN DAAN. *(Overlapping.)* A real Hanukkah in the end!

MR. FRANK. One last thing.

ANNE. What?

MR. FRANK. *(His hands behind his back.)* One present. Just one.

ANNE and MARGOT. *(Crowding around him.)* Who for? Show us!

MR. FRANK. For your mother. For tonight. *(He holds out a small package wrapped in newspaper and tied with string. Smiling, excited, Mrs. Frank unwraps it, takes out a delicate antique silver music box.)*

MRS. FRANK. *(Her eyes filling with tears.)* The music box … Otto. How did you —

MR. FRANK. I saved it for you. I was hoping we wouldn't be here till Hanukkah, but I brought it just in case.

MRS. FRANK. *(Caressing it lightly.)* This goes all the way back to my great-grandmother. *(To her daughters.)* Your father's an angel for saving it. *(Margot and Anne are silent, watching their parents embrace.)*

MRS. VAN DAAN. *(To her husband.)* Why didn't you save anything of mine?

MR. VAN DAAN. *(Leaning over her, tender.)* I saved you, didn't I?

MRS. FRANK. Listen. *(She places the music box on the table, lovingly lifts the blue velvet-lined lid. We hear the melody of "Ma-oz Tzur." Clustered around Mrs. Frank and the music box, the others listen as the melody continues. Peter comes out of his room, holding a bulge in his coat, dangling Mouschi's present before it.)*

PETER. Look! Mouschi loves his present.

MR. DUSSEL. *(Hiding behind a chair.)* Peter! He'll give me asthma!

MR. VAN DAAN. What's the matter with you? Get that cat out of here.

PETER. Cat? What cat? *(He pulls a towel from his coat, holds it high. Everyone laughs.)*

MR. DUSSEL. *(Wheezing unconvincingly.)* It doesn't have to be the cat. His clothes are enough.

MR. VAN DAAN. Don't worry. We're getting rid of it.

MR. DUSSEL. Finally. Finally you listen to me.

MR. VAN DAAN. I'm not doing it for you, Dussel. I'm just sick of those damn fleas. Out he goes.

ANNE. Mr. van Daan, you can't do that.

MARGOT. That's Peter's cat. Peter loves that cat.

PETER. If he goes, I go.

MR. VAN DAAN. So go. Go.

MRS. VAN DAAN. You're not going and the cat's not going. Put the towel away. Sit down, Mr. Dussel. It's Hanukkah. A time for celebration. Girls, sing the song.

MARGOT and ANNE. *(Smiling, shy, sing.)*

    Ma-oz tzur ye-shu-a-si
    Le-cha naw-eh lisha bayah
    Ti-kon beis te-fi-la-si
    Ve-shum to-daw —

(A sudden crash of something below the Annex. A dog barks. They freeze in horror. Mr. Frank takes off his shoes, turns off the lamp, goes to the stairs. The others take off their shoes. The dog barks again. Silence. The sound of footsteps on the stairs, approaching the Annex.)

ANNE. *(A whisper.)* Oh God. *(No one moves. In the silence, we hear them breathing. There is a rattling at the bookcase. Again. All breathing stops. Mr. Frank signals Peter to turn off the hanging lamp. Peter turns it off. In the dim candlelight, he knocks over a chair. The others cringe. The sound of feet running down the stairs.)*

MR. VAN DAAN. *(Under his breath.)* God Almighty! *(The footsteps recede. To Mr. Frank, in a whisper.)* Do you hear anything?

MR. FRANK. *(Listening carefully. Whispering.)* I think they've gone.

MRS. VAN DAAN. *(A whisper.)* The Gestapo?

MR. VAN DAAN. If it were the Gestapo, they'd be up here by now.

MR. FRANK. Maybe it was a thief.

MRS. VAN DAAN. We've got to do something.

MR. VAN DAAN. There's nothing to do. *(Mr. Frank holds up his hand for them to be quiet. Complete silence, as they strain to hear any sound from below.)*

MR. FRANK. I'm going down. *(He starts down the stairs.)*

MARGOT. *(Running toward him.)* No, Papa! They could still be there.

MRS. FRANK. *(As Mr. van Daan pulls Margot back.)* Margot, come back here!

MRS. VAN DAAN. *(Quietly hysterical.)* Maybe we can buy them off. Where's our money, Putti?

MR. VAN DAAN. Keep still.

MRS. VAN DAAN. *(A whispered panic.)* And wait till they drag us away? Do something!

MR. VAN DAAN. Will you keep still! *(He half lifts her up, makes her sit down.)*

ANNE. *(Unable to stand the silence.)* Someone get Papa.

MR. VAN DAAN. Quiet!

PETER. I'll go.

MR. VAN DAAN. Sit down.

ANNE. Please. Please go.

MR. VAN DAAN. Quiet! Everyone! *(The sound of footsteps on the stairs. They wait, rigid. Mr. Frank appears. Anne and Margot rush to him, hold him tight.)*

MR. FRANK. It was a thief.

MR. DUSSEL. How do you know?

MR. FRANK. He took the cash box, ran off so fast he left the front door wide open. The noise must have scared him away. *(As Mrs. Frank turns on a light.)* The danger's passed. We're safe.

MR. DUSSEL. Maybe. But we're in even greater danger now.

MR. FRANK. Mr. Dussel. Please.

MR. DUSSEL. *(Pointing at Peter.)* Now someone knows we're up here.

MR. VAN DAAN. Why are you pointing at him? It was an accident. It could have happened to any one of us.

MRS. VAN DAAN. *(Quiet.)* You mean to tell me a thief is going to go to the police and say "I was robbing a place the other night and I heard this noise above my head?" You think a thief is going to say that?

MR. DUSSEL. Yes. I do.

MRS. VAN DAAN. Well, you're crazy.

MR. DUSSEL. I think someday he'll get caught and make a bargain with the police. If they let him off, he'll tell them where some Jews are hiding. Maybe they'll even reward him. Seven and a half guilders a Jew. *(Silence.)*

ANNE. *(Terrified.)* We can't stay here anymore! Please, Papa. Let's go. Let's just go!

MRS. VAN DAAN. Go?

MR. VAN DAAN. Where would we go?

MRS. FRANK. Into the street?

MR. FRANK. No one's leaving. We can't panic. If we panic, we're lost. We've survived here for six months together. We're going on. Margot. Anne. The song. Please. *(Margot and Anne hesitate, then falteringly begin to sing.)*

MARGOT and ANNE. *Ma-oz tzur ye-shu-a-si*

EVERYONE. *(Slowly joining in, some humming, some singing the words.)*

> *Le-cha naw-eh lisha bayah*
> *Ti-kon beis te-fi-la-si*
> *Ve-shum to-daw*
> *n-zaw-bei-ach*
> *L'et takhin matbe'ach*
> *Mitzar hammnabe'* —

(Margot suddenly breaks down, takes off her glasses, sobbing silently. Mrs. Frank rushes to her. The others stop singing, move even closer, as Anne speaks directly to us.)

ANNE. Sometimes I see myself alone in a dungeon, without Father and Mother, or I'm roaming the streets, or the Annex is on fire, or they come in the middle of the night to take us away, and I know it could all happen soon. *(The members of the Annex linger together, shaking hands, embracing.)* I see the eight of us in the Annex as if we were a patch of blue sky threatened by menacing black clouds. We're surrounded by darkness and danger, and in our desperate search for a way out we keep bumping into each other. *(Mr. Dussel slips into the W.C. The two families separate — the van Daans with Peter go into their room, Mrs. Frank and Margot into Anne's room. Mr. Frank, the last to leave, holds Anne close to him. She remains, alone.)* We look at the fighting below and the peace and beauty above, but we're cut off by the dark mass of clouds and can go neither up nor down. It looms before us, an impenetrable wall. I can only cry out and implore, "Open wide. Let us out!" *(There is a sob from Margot. Anne rushes to her. The two families cling to each other. The house lights come up, as the light on the stage slowly dims.)*

End of Act One

ACT TWO

ANNE. *(At her desk, her diary before her, speaking directly out.)* Saturday, January first, 1944. Another new year has begun and we're in the middle of the great terror known as winter. We've been here one year, five months, and twenty-five days. We're all thinner, paler and a lot hungrier. We've been plagued by medical problems — someone's always suffering from something — and although we can't call a doctor, our favorite dentist is never too far away. *(A terrified shriek. Light comes up on Mrs. van Daan, wearing her fur coat, huddled in a chair, as Mr. Dussel bends over her with a tooth scraper. Peter acts as his assistant. Mrs. Frank, in a thick sweater and fingerless gloves, sits next to Margot, who wears Mr. Frank's scarf — the gift from Anne — around her throat. It is late afternoon on a cold winter day.)*

MR. DUSSEL. I'm almost done, Mrs. van Daan. If you can just hold on a little longer.

MRS. VAN DAAN. How can I? You're killing me.

MR. DUSSEL. If you'd stop complaining, perhaps I could finish sooner.

MRS. VAN DAAN. All right, all right. I'll try. *(Silence as Mr. Dussel continues working. Mrs. van Daan lets out a particularly piercing shriek, flails about wildly.)*

MR. DUSSEL. Mrs. van Daan, please! You've got my instrument stuck in your tooth.

MRS. VAN DAAN. *(Almost incomprehensible.)* Is that my fault? Pull it out! *(She lashes out in all directions, moaning in pain.)*

MR. DUSSEL. Stop moving! You're making it go in even further. *(Pushing him away, she finally yanks it out herself.)*

MRS. VAN DAAN. There. Look. *I* got it. *(Mr. Dussel comes closer, finishes working on Mrs. van Daan's mouth.)*

ANNE. I'm lucky. I've been healthy. In fact, I've been growing! So much I can't fit into my shoes anymore, not to speak of anything else. And there's another change — something happening inside me. Each time I get my period (and it's only been three times), I have the feeling that, despite the pain, I have a sweet secret. And I long for the time I'll feel that secret again. Sometimes, when I lie in bed at night, I feel a terrible urge to touch my breasts and listen to the beating of my heart. Once when I spent the night at Jopie's, I could no longer restrain my curiosity about her body, which she always kept hidden from me. I asked her if, as proof of our friendship, we could touch each other's breasts. She refused. I also had a terrible desire to kiss her, which I did. *(Mr. Frank comes into Anne's room with Margot and Mrs. Frank. Mrs. Frank watches Mr. Frank measure Margot and Anne against the door as Anne continues.)* Every time I see a female nude, such as the *Venus* in my art history book, I go into ecstasy. Sometimes I find them so exquisite I have to struggle to hold back my tears. *(A pause.)* And there's something else. Peter ... Whenever he looks at me with those eyes ... *(The sound of the buzzer.)*

MR. VAN DAAN. Miep! *(They all hurry into the main room as Miep comes up the stairs, carrying a ficelle [a knitted bag] and a cake on a plate covered with a napkin.)*

MRS. FRANK. Happy New Year, Miep!

MIEP. Happy New Year!

MRS. FRANK. You really should have this day to yourself, but we love that you've come.

ANNE. Oh Miep, you smell like the wind!

MIEP. Anne — how are you?

MR. DUSSEL. I wonder if you'd mind taking this letter. For Charlotte. For the New Year.

MIEP. Of course.

MR. VAN DAAN. Miepchen! *(Hopeful, he mimes smoking a cigarette. She shakes her head.)*

MIEP. Feeling any better, Margot?

MARGOT. A little.

MIEP. *(Removing the napkin from the cake.)* Maybe this will make you feel better yet.

MRS. VAN DAAN. Putti — look! The cake! The cake!

MR. VAN DAAN. Cake. I'll get the plates.

ANNE. Is it your special spice cake?

MIEP. *(Laughing.)* Spice cake, exactly. Your favorite.

MR. FRANK. Everyone's favorite.

MRS. FRANK. Spice cake. What a treat! You must have used up all your rations for the week.

MRS. VAN DAAN. How sweet! And look — she wrote "Peace in 1944."

MR. DUSSEL. Last year it was "Peace in 1943."

MIEP. Well, it has to come sometime, doesn't it?

MR. DUSSEL. Let's pray it will.

MR. VAN DAAN. Here's the knife, Petronella. Now, how many of us are there?

MIEP. None for me, thank you.

MR. FRANK. Oh, but you must.

MR. VAN DAAN. Well, that leaves seven.

MR. DUSSEL. Eight! Eight! The same number it always is.

MR. VAN DAAN. I took it for granted Margot wouldn't have any.

ANNE. Why not?

MRS. FRANK. I don't think a piece of cake would harm her.

MR. VAN DAAN. I don't want her to start coughing again. Eight, eight — all right, eight!

MR. DUSSEL. And please, Mrs. Frank should cut the cake. *(Silence, as they all look at him.)* Mrs. Frank divides things ... better.

MRS. VAN DAAN. What are you saying? Don't I always give everyone exactly the same?

MR. DUSSEL. Yes, yes. Everyone always gets exactly the same. *(As Mrs. van Daan starts to cut the cake.)* Except Mr. van Daan always gets a little bit more.

MRS. VAN DAAN. *(Throwing down the knife.)* Now just a minute —

MR. FRANK. *(Taking Mrs. van Daan's arm.)* Please, please! Miep, you see how a little spice cake goes to our heads?

MR. VAN DAAN. *(Handing Mrs. Frank the knife.)* Here, Mrs. Frank. You cut.

MR. FRANK. It looks delicious, Miep.

MRS. FRANK. *(Dividing the cake into tiny, even pieces.)* Oh, that smell! Miep, you're sure you won't have a piece?

MIEP. No, thank you. I have to leave in a minute. *(Mr. van Daan passes out the plates with the cake. For moments, they all eat blissfully.)*

MR. VAN DAAN. *(Groaning with pleasure.)* Ah, Miep. Miepchen. Jan is lucky to get a woman who can bake like this.

ANNE. Jan! Tell us about Jan.

MIEP. Jan's taking me to a party tonight.

ANNE. A party! Oh Miep! Remember everything so you can tell us about it tomorrow.

MARGOT. Everyone you dance with —

MIEP. Jan. Only with Jan. *(As they laugh.)* Oh, I seem to have forgotten something ... for someone. *(Facing Anne, she holds out the ficelle.)*

ANNE. Me? *(She looks into the ficelle, throws her arms around Miep.)*

MRS. VAN DAAN. What? What is it? Come on. I can't stand the suspense. *(Everyone watches as Anne takes a pair of red leather high-heeled shoes from the ficelle. She slips off her shoes. Mrs. Frank helps her put on the red ones.)*

MRS. FRANK. Oh my ... Miep, where did you find them?

MR. VAN DAAN. You can't even get a slipper on the black market these days.

MRS. VAN DAAN. *(Eating her cake.)* Look. They match! Incredible. *(Taking a step, Anne totters, almost falls. They laugh, as Anne, awkward and graceful, moves around the room in her first pair of high-heeled shoes.)*

MR. FRANK. All grown up! Ready for Hollywood.

MIEP. Enjoy them, Anne. *(She starts to leave.)* And don't worry. I'll give you all a full report tomorrow.

MR. VAN DAAN. Miep. There's something I'd like you to do for me. *(Mrs. van Daan gets up.)*

MRS. VAN DAAN. *(Taking her fur coat.)* What? What are you talking about?

MR. VAN DAAN. You know what I'm talking about. *(He moves toward her.)*

MIEP. What is it?

PETER. He wants to sell her fur coat.

MRS. VAN DAAN. *(Moving away, clutching her coat. Quiet.)* No, Putti. Don't do this to me. This is my coat. I've had this coat for seventeen years. My father gave me this coat. You have no right. Don't you dare! Let go.

MR. VAN DAAN. You have to give it up.

MRS. VAN DAAN. Let go of it. Please.

MR. VAN DAAN. You can't hold on to a fur coat when people are in such desperate need of warm clothing. *(To the others.)* Besides we're broke. We've been running out of money for months. *(To his wife, gently.)* I have to sell it. *(Taking the coat from her hands, he gives it to Miep, who starts for the stairs. Mrs. Frank follows Miep down a few steps, stops. At the bottom step Miep turns back. Mrs. Frank is staring at her.)*

MIEP. *(Coming back up the stairs.)* Mrs. Frank?

MRS. FRANK. Oh Miep. I remember when a New Year was something to look forward to.

MIEP. Mrs. Frank. You mustn't give up hope.

MRS. FRANK. There's no hope to be had. I know that. I knew it the night Hitler came to power, when that voice came screaming out of the radio. I sat there paralyzed. And now in London, what is the Dutch Queen doing? What are they all doing? They're not even *mentioning* the word Jew. The trains are still leaving. Why don't they bomb the tracks? *(Miep is silent.)* I can't talk about this with the others, Miep.

MIEP. I understand, Mrs. Frank.

MRS. FRANK. I know they're making plans, counting the days till the war is over, but I have to tell you … I feel the end will never come. *(Pause.)* Sometimes … sometimes I want to give myself up.

MIEP. Forgive me, Mrs. Frank, but you must try and take things a little easier. They need you. The children need you.

MRS. FRANK. I'm ashamed to feel this way. I know you and Mr. Kraler have it just as hard.

MIEP. No, Mrs. Frank. We don't.

MRS. FRANK. Thank you. For listening to me. *(At the table, Mr. Dussel studies French with Anne, Peter works on Math, Mrs. van Daan busies herself in the kitchen as her husband watches.)*

MR. DUSSEL. *"Non, non, ce n'est pas ce que tu penses."* *(He pronounces "penses" incorrectly, rhyming with "sense.")*

ANNE. *(Correcting him.)* "*Penses*," Mr. Dussel. "*Penses.*" From *penser.* To think. *(He puts his head in his hands.) Ce que vous ne faites pas beaucoup.*

MR. DUSSEL. What?

ANNE. *Ce que vous ne faites pas.*

MR. DUSSEL. You're going too fast.

ANNE. *Oui. Je sais.*

MR. DUSSEL. *(A pause. Looking up, smiling.) Je sais.* I know that one.

ANNE. *Bon. Continuons. La page suivante, s'il vous plait.*

MRS. VAN DAAN. I just don't understand. I would never … *never* have done anything like that to you.

MR. VAN DAAN. The coat was seventeen years old, for God's sake! Those skins had definitely seen their day.

MRS. VAN DAAN. That's not the point and you know it.

MR. VAN DAAN. I know we need the money. We have no money — can you get that through your head?

PETER. Don't talk to her like that.

MRS. VAN DAAN. You've never understood. Anything.

MR. VAN DAAN. Oh God, here we go again.

MRS. VAN DAAN. That coat was the last thing. A whole world gone.

MR. VAN DAAN. Well you've still got us, haven't you?

MRS. VAN DAAN. You took the last memory of my father away.

MR. VAN DAAN. *(Rising, banging the table.)* Do we have to hear about your father again? If you hadn't been so attached to your father, your coat, the apartment with all our goddamned possessions, we'd be in America by now!

PETER. It's not her fault.

MRS. VAN DAAN. Oh please. It was you too, you know. You didn't want to —

MR. VAN DAAN. I only stayed because of you! Believe me, I knew which way the wind was blowing.

MRS. VAN DAAN. Oh. Sure. You always know everything.

PETER. Mother. Please. Stop.

MR. VAN DAAN. Your mother will never listen.

ANNE. *(Coming over to Mrs. van Daan. Quiet.)* If I could just say one thing.

MRS. VAN DAAN. No, you cannot! You say too much already and it's none of your business anyway. *(Anne retreats to her room in tears.)*

PETER. You shouldn't have said that, Mother.

MRS. VAN DAAN. *(Choked.)* What?

PETER. You hurt her feelings.

MRS. VAN DAAN. Oh. Well. I apologize. All right? I apologize — to everyone! *(She goes into the W.C., slamming the door behind her. Peter picks up Anne's cake and goes to her room.)*

PETER. You left this.

ANNE. *(Hiding her tears.)* Thank you. *(Peter starts to leave, turns back, stands there awkwardly.)*

PETER. I ... I'm sorry for what happened in there. I wish I could have said something. But they make me feel so ... I can't stand it when they ... Sometimes I wish I didn't belong to them at all! I just hope I never turn out like them.

ANNE. You won't. I know it.

PETER. Like him. What if I'm like him?

ANNE. You're not. Believe me.

PETER. All I can say is if it wasn't for you ... I mean ... You ... *(Blurting it out.)* You're always a big help to me.

ANNE. I am? How?

PETER. When you're cheerful it ... well ... it keeps me from being depressed. *(Mr. Dussel opens the door, looks from Peter to Anne, backs out.)*

ANNE. I'm not always so cheerful, you know ... inside.

PETER. Really?

ANNE. It's hard. If you want to cry or something. There's nowhere to go.

PETER. It's easier for me, I guess. When there's a fight ... you know, with my parents ... I just duck into my room.

ANNE. You're lucky you have a room of your own.

PETER. Well, at least you can talk to your parents.

ANNE. Not really. I never discuss anything serious with Mother. She just doesn't understand. I can talk about everything with Father ... except Mother. I don't think you can really ... really be intimate with someone if they hold something back, do you?

PETER. I think your father's terrific.

ANNE. He likes you too.

PETER. *(Looking up quickly, blushing.)* You think so?

ANNE. I can tell from the little things he says. *(She pauses.)* It's funny, isn't it?

PETER. What?

ANNE. Well, we've been living here for almost a year and a half and this ... this is the first time we've really talked.

PETER. I know what you mean.

ANNE. You know something, Peter?

PETER. What?

ANNE. I ... I've never really had a friend. Someone I could truly confide in. *(She is still, looking at him. He smiles.)*

PETER. Me neither. *(A moment. Suddenly.)* Smile for me.

ANNE. Why?

PETER. You have dimples when you smile.

ANNE. Dimples — the only mark of beauty I possess.

PETER. That's not true. You're pretty.

ANNE. Me? *(Peter nods.)*

PETER. Yes. *(Quiet.)* You. *(Anne looks down. A pause. She looks up, a dazzling smile. Moments pass. They smile at each other. Still looking at her, Peter starts to go, almost trips, catches himself, leaves. Anne continues to smile. Chopin's Nocturne A-flat major, Op. 32, No. 2 begins over the BBC dinner concert, as light brightens on Anne joyously dancing around the table in the main room. Lost in a blissful reverie, she is unseen by the others, who are getting ready for supper. But even they seem transformed by Anne's happiness, as the simple household activities — setting the table, the worn tablecloth ballooning out as it is put down, bringing in the plates, laying the silverware — all become a kind of ritual.)*

ANNE. *(Directly to us.)* The sun is shining, the sky a deep blue, there's a magnificent breeze, and I'm longing — so longing — for everything! I walk from room to room, breathe through the crack in the window frame, feel my heart beating as if to say, "Can't you fulfill this longing at last?" I long for every boy, and to Peter I want to shout, "Say something, don't just smile at me all the time, touch me, so I can get that delicious feeling inside." I feel spring within me, I feel spring awakening, I feel it in my entire body and soul. I'm utterly confused, don't know what to read, to write, to do. I only know ... I am longing ... *(Anne joins them as they sit down at the table. Mrs. Frank and Mrs. van Daan serve a supper of kale and potatoes.)*

MR. VAN DAAN. What is it tonight?

MRS. VAN DAAN. Don't ask.

MR. VAN DAAN. I have to. I have to be prepared.

MR. DUSSEL. My God, I can't eat this again! Pickles, kale, and rotten potatoes — every night for weeks now.

MR. VAN DAAN. Something wrong, Mr. Dussel? You try cooking for a change, instead of insulting my wife.

MR. FRANK. I think you prepared the kale very well, Mrs. van Daan. I don't know how you do it.

MRS. VAN DAAN. Mr. Frank. Always the soul of politeness.

MR. FRANK. Every night another miracle. *(Mr. Dussel hastily gets up from the table, lurches toward the W.C.)*

MR. VAN DAAN. Careful, Mr. Dussel! We don't want to clog the pipes like last week.

MRS. VAN DAAN. Putti, please.

MRS. FRANK. You're not eating, Margot. *(Margot is still.)* Eat. You have to eat.

MARGOT. I'm not hungry.

MR. VAN DAAN. If she doesn't want it, Peter will eat it.

MR. FRANK. Come, Margot. Just take a bite.

MARGOT. *(Giving Peter her plate.)* I can't. I just can't.

MRS. VAN DAAN. She eats like a bird. Look at her. Every day a smaller bird. Margot, I'm doing the best I can.

MARGOT. I'm sorry, Mrs. van Daan. I just —

MRS. VAN DAAN. Anne's eating. Peter's eating.

MARGOT. How do you do it, Anne?

ANNE. I pretend it's delicious, don't look at it, and before I know it, it's gone.

MR. FRANK. Very wise, Anneke.

PETER. I eat because I'm hungry. *(Silence. Anne laughs — a tender flirtatious laugh. Mrs. van Daan looks from her to Peter.)*

MR. FRANK. You've got to force yourself, Margot. You're too thin.

MR. VAN DAAN. She's not the only one. We're all famished. *(Silence, except for their spoons scraping their bowls.)*

MARGOT. Will this war ever be over?

MRS. VAN DAAN. This war would be over a lot sooner if the goddamned British would start the invasion.

MR. VAN DAAN. Please. Not tonight.

MR. FRANK. The British are fighting for their lives.

MR. VAN DAAN. They'll do something when the time is right.

MRS. VAN DAAN. When we're dead and buried, you mean. It's amazing how strong those Germans are.

MR. VAN DAAN. Oh, it's amazing. Those Germans are so strong they're going to win the war — is that what you're saying?

MRS. VAN DAAN. They might. They very well might — if the British don't get moving.

MR. VAN DAAN. They're moving, for crying out loud! Three thousand tons of bombs dropped on Hamburg last Sunday — isn't that enough for you?

MRS. VAN DAAN. No.

MR. VAN DAAN. How many bombs do you need?

MRS. VAN DAAN. *(Rising.)* Enough so we don't have to worry about *going to Poland! (Margot, gagging, leaps up, rushes to the W.C.)*

MRS. FRANK. *(Following her.)* Hurry up, Mr. Dussel! Margot's waiting!

MR. FRANK. *(Overlapping.)* Mr. Dussel!

MRS. VAN DAAN. *(Overlapping.)* For God's sake, hurry!

PETER. *(Overlapping.)* She can't wait any longer!

ANNE. *(Overlapping.)* Please, Mr. Dussel! Come on!

MR. VAN DAAN. Mr. Dussel, the line is forming *again.*

MR. DUSSEL. *(Emerging from the W.C.)* You think I like spending my life in there? *(The piercing sound of the buzzer. They freeze. Mr. Kraler appears on the stairs.)*

MR. FRANK. Mr. Kraler!

MR. KRALER. I'm sorry to come at this hour. But something's happened.

MRS. VAN DAAN. *(Shaken.)* What?

MR. KRALER. I must ask you all to be more careful. More quiet.

MR. FRANK. What's happened?

MR. KRALER. A man in the storeroom — a few days ago he

asked me, "What do you hear from Mr. Frank?" I said I'd heard a rumor you were in Switzerland. He said he'd heard that too, but thought I might know something more. And then today, signing some invoices, I looked up and saw him staring at the bookcase.

MRS. FRANK. *(Almost inaudible.)* My God.

MR. KRALER. He said he thought he remembered a door there. Then he said he wanted more money. Ten more guilders a month.

MR. VAN DAAN. Blackmail. *(Mrs. Frank wanders out, goes into Anne's room.)*

MR. FRANK. Ten guilders? Very modest blackmail.

MR. DUSSEL. It's just the beginning.

MR. FRANK. What did you tell him?

MR. KRALER. I said I had to think about it. Should I pay him the money? Take a chance on firing him, or —

MR. DUSSEL. For God's sake, pay him the money!

MR. FRANK. Offer him half. We'll find out if it's blackmail or not.

MR. KRALER. Listen. Maybe he knows nothing. But it's more dangerous out there every day. No one can be trusted. You must be quiet. Quiet! *(Silence, as they all look at him. Anne, who has noticed her mother leaving, goes out.)* I'll offer him half then.

MR. FRANK. *(Shaking his hand.)* Thank you, Mr. Kraler.

MR. KRALER. We'll hope for the best.

MR. VAN DAAN. *(As he leaves.)* Thank you. *(Mrs. Frank, in tears, sits at Anne's desk. Anne, at the door, watches her.)*

ANNE. Mother. Please. Don't be upset. *(Mrs. Frank wipes her tears away.)* I can't bear it ... seeing you this way.

MRS. FRANK. I'll be all right, Anneke. You go back to supper. *(Slowly Anne sits down on the bed.)*

ANNE. I'd rather stay here. With you. *(For moments Mrs. Frank is still. Then she goes to Anne, tenderly strokes her hair. The light dims on them both and comes up on Mrs. van Daan in the W.C., looking at herself in the mirror. She touches her face. Hurriedly, silently she pulls the door shut. Light comes up on Peter, getting dressed in his room, as we hear the end of a song on the BBC.)*

BROADCAST. *(V.O.)* And now, from London, a message from the Dutch Minister of Education, Mr. Gerrit Bolkestein.

BOLKESTEIN. *(V.O.)* History cannot be written on the basis of official documents alone. If our descendants are to understand what we as a nation have endured during these years, we need simple, every-day pieces — a diary, letters from a forced laborer in Germany ...

(Light instantly reveals Anne, sitting at her desk in a slip, her diary before her.)

ANNE. *(Overlapping, speaking out.)* I can't believe it! Did he really say "a diary"? I'll start revising it tomorrow! Maybe one day I could even publish a novel. *The Secret Annex* — based on my diary! *(A pause.)* Unless you write yourself, you can't know how wonderful it is. When I write I shake off all my cares. But I want to achieve more than that. I want to be useful and bring enjoyment to all people, even those I've never met. I want to go on living even after my death! *(Light comes up on Mr. and Mrs. Frank and Mr. and Mrs. van Daan playing cards in the main room, as a fierce whispered argument goes on between Margot and Mr. Dussel, impatient to get into his room. As Margot comes in, Anne quickly puts her diary away, picks up a comb and starts combing her hair.)*

MARGOT. Mr. Dussel is getting awfully impatient out there.

ANNE. *(Continuing to get dressed.)* Let him! I'm always waiting for him.

MARGOT. *(Watching her.)* Are you going up to the attic with Peter again? *(Anne is silent.)* You've already spent so much time there today.

ANNE. I went up exactly twice. Once to practice French together and once to get the potatoes for supper.

MARGOT. But you know Mrs. van Daan. She's got a comment for every little thing.

ANNE. She can't help herself. It's in her nature. I don't think it's Mrs. van Daan that's upsetting you. *(She puts on the red shoes.)*

MARGOT. I'm not upset.

ANNE. You're not jealous? Of Peter and me? *(Margot is still.)* I'd be insanely jealous if it were you instead of me.

MARGOT. Yes, I imagine you would be. But I'm not.

ANNE. Aren't you, Margot? Tell me the truth.

MARGOT. Who wouldn't want someone to visit every night, have deep serious conversations with … and who knows what else. Yes, I'm jealous. But not of you and Peter. I'd just like someone of my own. I'm happy you have someone.

ANNE. You mean it?

MARGOT. *(Taking Anne's hand.)* I want you to have a good time tonight. Every night. You've already missed out on so much here.

ANNE. Oh Margot, you're such a generous person! Anyway, there's nothing to be jealous of. We don't *do* anything! *(They both laugh. And it's suddenly quiet.)* He's never even kissed me.

MARGOT. The kiss will come.

ANNE. I'm not sure I want it to.

MARGOT. *(Grinning.)* Oh, you do. I know you. You can't help yourself. *(She gives Anne a little push.)* It's in your nature. *(Anne pushes her back. They giggle, then look at each other, silent. As Anne turns to go, Margot picks up the comb.)* Wait. Let me fix your hair. *(Quickly she combs Anne's luxuriant hair, turns her around, looks at her lovingly.)* There. Now you're ready. *(Anne smiles. Gently, Margot pushes her out. She stands still for a moment, then quietly folds Anne's clothes.)*

MR. DUSSEL. I presume I may finally get back into my room.

ANNE. *Our* room, dear Mr. Dussel. And yes, you may return.

MR. DUSSEL. Thank you so much. *(Anne curtseys.)*

MRS. FRANK. Anne. Again?

MRS. VAN DAAN. Again … and look at her.

MRS. FRANK. *(To Anne.)* It's cold in the attic. You'd better bundle up.

MRS. VAN DAAN. *(As Anne goes into her parents room for a sweater.)* In my day it was the boys who called on the girls.

MR. FRANK. Young people like to feel they have secrets. The attic's the only place they can talk.

MRS. VAN DAAN. Talk? That's not what they called it in my day.

MR. VAN DAAN. I think a little romance may be developing in our little Annex.

MRS. VAN DAAN. *(As Anne comes back.)* If we're here much longer, we may even have a little Annex wedding.

MRS. FRANK. *(Suddenly facing the van Daans.)* Frankly, I can't stand this stupid chatter another minute! *(Mr. Frank and the van Daans stare at her. Anne flashes her a grateful smile.)* Anne! Don't forget to be down by nine. *(Anne and Peter go up to the attic, Anne stumbling in her red shoes.)*

ANNE. They're so old-fashioned! I guess they don't realize how much more advanced we are. *(The van Daans return to their card game, Mr. Dussel comes out of the W.C., Mrs. Frank mends a skirt, Mr. Frank and Margot read together.)*

PETER. You look nice.

ANNE. Really?

PETER. I like the shoes. I've always liked the shoes. *(Anne holds out her feet.)*

ANNE. Miep always does everything just right.

PETER. She likes you a lot.

ANNE. I love her. But I hate having to ask for absolutely every-thing. Doesn't it make you miserable to be so dependent on people?
PETER. *(Lighting a candle on top of a crate.)* I'm not miserable ... anymore. I mean ... even bumping into you on the stairs sometimes I feel ... *(He stops.)*
ANNE. I feel the same. *(Peter holds out a chair for her.)*
PETER. *(Grinning.)* You've changed. I used to think you were a real pain in the neck.
ANNE. My life before seems so unreal — nothing to do with who I am now. I see myself then as an utterly superficial girl. I wouldn't go back to being her for the world.
PETER. You sure know a lot about yourself, don't you? I guess it comes from all that writing you do.
ANNE. If I didn't — I mean write what I think, what I feel — I'd suffocate! *(He is silent, staring at her.)* I want to be a *real* writer one day. I know I can write — I'm my harshest critic — but who knows if I truly have talent or not. *(She pauses.)* What do *you* want to do?
PETER. *(Pulling up a crate, sitting down.)* I don't know. Some job that doesn't take much brains. Maybe if I had your drive —
ANNE. That's ridiculous.
PETER. No. It's true. I'm a complete idiot.
ANNE. You're too hard on yourself.
PETER. I didn't have much going for me on the outside.
ANNE. But don't you miss — Oh Peter, I miss so many things ... *(Going to the window.)* Sometimes I dream I'm back in our old apartment. I wake up and wonder ... why can't I run outside? *(She stops.)* Oh! You *can* see the moon from here — just like you said. How beautiful! *(Turning back into the attic.)* Look at our attic. The moonlight coming in.
PETER. *(Coming up behind her.)* Are you cold?
ANNE. No. Well, maybe just a little.
PETER. *(Putting his jacket around her shoulders.)* Here. *(Slowly he lifts his hand, touches a lock of her hair. She remains still.)*
ANNE. *(Turning toward him.)* Peter ... have you ever kissed a girl?
PETER. I guess so.
ANNE. You have? When?
PETER. It wasn't a big deal or anything.
ANNE. Tell me.
PETER. On my birthday. I was blindfolded. I don't even know who the girl was. *(Anne laughs.)*

ANNE. *(In a rush.)* There's nothing wrong with being kissed or any-thing. Though I'm sure Margot would never kiss a boy unless she were engaged to him. And I know Mother never touched a man before she met Pim. My girlfriends would say, "Anne, how shocking!" But who cares what they'd say anyway? Everything's different now ... here.

PETER. You called it our attic before. Do you really think it's ours?

ANNE. *(Quiet.)* I do.

PETER. You won't let them stop you coming here, will you?

ANNE. No. I promise. *(A pause.)* Maybe I'll bring one of my stories and read it to you sometime.

PETER. You'll come tomorrow night?

ANNE. If you want me to.

PETER. I do.

MR. FRANK. *(Calling up to the attic.)* It's 9:05!

ANNE. *(Smiling.)* I will then. *(She turns to go. Silence. Behind her, Peter holds his breath, quickly, awkwardly kisses the back of her head. She doesn't move. Suddenly she turns, throws her arms around his neck, kisses him on the mouth. The kiss grows longer. In a daze they embrace. Anne gazes at him, enraptured, then tears down the stairs without looking back. Peter blows out the candle. In the main room everyone turns to look at Anne. For a moment she stares at all of them, smiles tremulously, then rushes into the W.C., slamming the door behind her. Darkness. Rauter, chief of the local police and the SS in the occupied Netherlands, is heard voiceover.)*

RAUTER. *(V.O.)* All Jews must be out of German-occupied countries before July first. The province of Utrecht will be cleansed of Jews between April first and May first, the provinces of North and South Holland, including Amsterdam, immediately thereafter. A faster pace evacuating the Jews will begin as we move them by train not once but twice a week, transporting 12,000 Jews a month. This is dirty work, but a mission of great historical purpose. When not a single Jew remains in the Netherlands, people will again walk freely in the streets. *(Night. Everyone is asleep. Abruptly Mrs. Frank sits up in bed.)*

MRS. FRANK. *(In a whisper.)* Otto. Listen. A rat!

MR. FRANK. Edith, please. Go back to sleep. *(He turns over. Mrs. Frank gets up, quietly creeps to the main room, stands still. There is a tiny crunching sound. In the darkness, a figure is faintly illuminated, crouched over, gnawing on something. Mrs. Frank moves closer, turns on the light. Trembling, Mr. van Daan jumps to his feet. He is clutching a piece of bread.)*

MRS. FRANK. My God, I don't believe it. The bread! He's stealing the bread!

MR. VAN DAAN. No, no. Quiet.

MR. FRANK. *(As everyone comes into the main room in their night-clothes.)* Hermann, for God's sake!

MRS. VAN DAAN. *(Sleepily opening her eyes.)* What is it? What's going on?

MRS. FRANK. Your husband. Stealing our bread!

MRS. VAN DAAN. That can't be. Putti, what are you doing?

MR. VAN DAAN. Never before! Never before!

MRS. FRANK. I don't believe you. If he steals once, he'll steal again. Every day I watch the children getting thinner. And he comes in the middle of the night and steals food that should go to them!

MR. VAN DAAN. *(His head in his hands.)* Oh my God. My God.

MR. FRANK. Edith. Please.

MARGOT. Mama, it's only one piece of bread.

MR. VAN DAAN. *(Putting the bread on the table. In a panic.)* Here. *(Mrs. Frank swats the bread away.)*

MRS. FRANK. *(Quiet.)* I want him to go.

MRS. VAN DAAN. Go? Go where?

MRS. FRANK. Anywhere.

MRS. VAN DAAN. You don't mean what you're saying.

MR. DUSSEL. It would be impossible for —

MR. FRANK. Edith, you know how upset you've been these past —

MRS. FRANK. That has nothing to do with it.

MR. FRANK. He couldn't help himself. It could happen to any one of us. *(He looks at Mr. van Daan.)* It won't happen again.

MR. VAN DAAN. Never. I promise.

MRS. FRANK. No! I can't take it with them here! They have to go.

MRS. VAN DAAN. You'd put us out on the street?

MRS. FRANK. There are other hiding places. Miep will find something. Don't worry about the money. I'll find you the money.

MRS. VAN DAAN. Mr. Frank, you said you'd never forget what my husband did for you.

MRS. FRANK. If my husband had any obligation to you, it's paid for.

MR. FRANK. For God's sake, Edith, I've never seen you like this!

ANNE. You can't throw Peter out! He hasn't done anything.

MRS. FRANK. Peter can stay.

PETER. I wouldn't feel right without my parents.

ANNE. Please, Mother. They'll be killed on the street!

MARGOT. Anne's right. You can't send them away.

MRS. FRANK. They can stay till Miep finds them a place. But we're switching rooms. I don't want him near the food.

MR. DUSSEL. Let's divide it up right now. *(He hurries to get a sack of potatoes.)*

MARGOT. We're not going to divide up some rotten potatoes.

MR. DUSSEL. *(Dividing the potatoes into piles.)* Mrs. Frank, Mr. Frank, Margot, Anne, Peter, Mrs. van Daan, Mr. van Daan, myself … Mrs. Frank, Mr. Frank —

MARGOT. *(Overlapping.)* Stop, Mr. Dussel! No more. No more! I beg you. Please. Don't! *(Mr. Dussel continues counting nonstop. In tears.)* I can't bear it!

MRS. FRANK. All this … all that's happening …

MR. FRANK. Enough! Margot. Mr. Dussel. Everyone — back in your rooms. Come, Edith. Mr. Dussel, I think the potatoes can wait. *(Mr. Dussel goes on counting. Tearing the sack from Mr. Dussel, the potatoes spilling:)* Just let them wait! *(He holds out his hand for Mrs. Frank. They all go back to their rooms. Peter and Mrs. van Daan pick up the scattered potatoes. Not looking at each other, Mr. and Mrs. van Daan move to their separate beds. The buzzer rings frantically, breaking the silence.)* Miep? At this hour? *(Miep runs up the stairs as everyone comes back into the main room.)*

MIEP. *(Out of breath.)* Everyone … everyone … the most wonderful, most incredible news!

MR. FRANK. What is it?

MIEP. *(Tears streaming down her cheeks.)* The invasion. The invasion has begun! *(They stare at her, unable to grasp what she is telling them.)* Did you hear me? The invasion! It's happening — right now! You can feel it in the streets — the excitement! *(Mrs. Frank begins to cry.)* I ran to tell you before the workmen got here. This is it. They've landed on the coast of Normandy!

PETER. The British?

MIEP. British, Americans … everyone! More than four thousand ships! Look — I brought a map. *(Quickly she unrolls a map of Normandy on the table.)*

MR. FRANK. *(Weeping, embracing his daughters.)* For over a year we've prayed for this moment.

MIEP. *(Pointing.)* Cherbourg. The first city. They're fighting for it now.

MR. DUSSEL. How many days will it take them from Normandy to the Netherlands?

MR. FRANK. *(Taking Mrs. Frank in his arms.)* Edith, what did I tell you.

MR. DUSSEL. *(Placing the potatoes on the map to hold it down as he checks the cities.)* Cherbourg. Caen. Pont-l'Évêque. Paris. And then … Amsterdam! *(Mr. van Daan breaks into a convulsive sob.)*

MRS. VAN DAAN. Putti.

MR. FRANK. Hermann, don't you hear? We're going to be free … soon. *(Mr. Dussel turns on the radio. Amidst much static, Eisenhower's voice is heard from his broadcast of June 6, 1944.)*

EISENHOWER. *(V.O.)* People of Western Europe, a landing was made this morning on the coast of France by troops of the Allied Expeditionary Force.

MR. FRANK. *(Wiping tears from his eyes.)* Listen. That's General Eisenhower. *(Anne pulls Margot down to her room.)*

EISENHOWER. *(V.O. fading away.)* I have this message for all of you. Although the initial assault may not have been made in your own country, the hour of your liberation is approaching.

ANNE. *(Hugging Margot.)* Home, Margot — can you believe it? We could be going home.

MARGOT. I don't even know what home would be like anymore. I can't imagine it — we've been away so long.

ANNE. Oh I can! I can imagine every little detail. To be outside again. The sky, Margot! To walk along the canal. To … everything! *(They sit on Anne's bed.)*

MARGOT. I'm afraid to let myself think about it. To have a real meal — *(They laugh together.)* It doesn't seem possible. Will anything taste the same? Look the same? *(More and more serious.)* I don't know if anything will ever … *be* the same again. How can we go back … really. *(Looking at Anne's wistful face.)* You know what I've decided? To be a nurse. For newborns. Go far, far away.

ANNE. How far?

MARGOT. Maybe … I don't know … Maybe to Palestine. *(Hugging Anne.)* Maybe you'll go back to school in October … September even. Wouldn't that be something, Anneke! *(They kiss each other, half laughing, half crying. Margot leaves, Anne gets into bed, as light comes up on Mrs. van Daan at the kitchen table. Mr. van Daan lies on his bed, disconsolate.)*

MRS. VAN DAAN. Putti? *(A pause.)* You know what I was just thinking? You won't believe this, but I was thinking about that first day we met, when you were buzzing around with the rest of the boys in Bremerhaven. I picked you out right away, you know. You were the one who made me laugh. And laugh … *(She laughs, full-throated, deep.)* That afternoon you took me out on the ferry, first you made me laugh and then you started to kiss me. And kiss me … And the kisses were even better than the laughter — remember? You gave me so many, the ferryman kept watching us and the ferry went off course, and then you made me laugh even more. When we got back, you had such a ravenous appetite you made that little restaurant open its doors and you ordered almost everything on the menu. "What an appetite!" the waiter kept saying. "The man can really eat!" *(She stands up, moves toward him.)* We'll go back on that ferry one day, Putti. I promise. It won't be long now. And soon I'll be cooking all your old favorites — sauerbraten with red cabbage, latkes with your cherished applesauce. We'll even go to Berkhof's for cream cakes! But in the meantime, Putti, if you're hungry, hold on to me. Oh Putti, please. Just hold on to me. *(They embrace … Darkness. Alone in her bed, Anne wakes with a start, her shadow, enormous, illuminated on the wall. She speaks out.)*

ANNE. Just as I was falling asleep, my friend Hanneli appeared, dressed in rags, her face thin and worn. She looked at me with such sadness in her eyes I could read the message in them: "Oh Anne, why have you deserted me? Help me, help me, rescue me from this hell!" If only I could. Why have I been chosen to live, and you to die? Oh Hanneli, Hanneli, if you ever return, I'll take you in, share everything I have with you. Are you still alive? I keep seeing your enormous eyes, keep seeing myself in your place. You're a reminder of what my fate might have been. *(Light comes up on Mrs. Frank on her knees, silently scrubbing the kitchen floor.)* What will we do if we're … no, I mustn't write that down. But the question won't go away. It looms before me in total absolute horror. *(A blue light. The chimney of the Annex is highlighted. A moment. Smoke begins to billow out of the chimney. Over the radio we hear a deep voice, contralto or baritone, singing the last verse of "Wenn dein Mütterlein" from Mahler's* Kindertotenlieder.*)*

BROADCAST. *(V.O.)*
Wenn dein Mütterlein
tritt zur Tür herein
Mit der Kerze Schimmer
ist es mir, als immer

Kämst du mit herein
huschtest hinterdrein
Als wie sonst ins Zimmer!
O du, des Vaters Zelle,
Ach, zu schnell
erloschner Freudenschein!

And so we come to the end of this broadcast from BBC Radio Europe. Till tomorrow, listeners, and we all know:

"No matter how hard the times,

And how heavy the separation,

We are once more a day closer to the liberation!"

(A bright sunlit morning. The attic is bathed in light. Peter and Margot, a crate of fresh strawberries between them, are picking them clean of stems and dirt, rinsing them in a bucket of water, preparing them for jam. Anne climbs up to the attic, joins them. Smiling, she grabs a handful of strawberries.)

ANNE. *(Mouth full.)* Strawberries! There's nothing I love more.

PETER. I can't understand you. Your mouth's too full.

MARGOT. I wouldn't talk — you haven't stopped eating since we came up.

PETER. You're the one who's eating! Look at you. You're all red.

ANNE. *(Laughing.)* Look at *you*! They're all over your shirt. *(Peter looks down, then up, as Anne chucks him under the chin. He hugs her lightly. They go back to cleaning and eating the berries.)*

PETER. Well, it's a lot better than those string beans yesterday.

MARGOT. Green, green, green — I thought they'd never end.

ANNE. Every string I pulled made me sure I never want to be just a housewife.

PETER. You never will be. *(Anne smiles as, in the main room, light comes up on the adults gathered around a plate of strawberries.)*

MRS. FRANK. *(Munching a strawberry.)* Ohh. I forgot how wonderful they are.

MR. VAN DAAN. Of course you forgot. We haven't seen a berry in two years.

MRS. VAN DAAN. Don't eat too many, Putti. Remember how sick you were last night from the kale soup.

MR. DUSSEL. I'm just worried there won't be any left for jam with those three up in the attic.

MR. FRANK. Mr. Dussel, you're such a worrier! Let the children enjoy themselves. *(Munching one himself.)* God, these are good. *(They settle down to a silent game of seven-card gin rummy, the plate of strawberries before them on the table. The only sounds are the shuffling, dealing and playing of the cards. A peaceful everyday scene.)*

ANNE. I'll tell you a secret … every night I think, "They're coming, they're coming — our liberators!"

PETER. I bet you'll both forget about me when you're back with all your old friends.

MARGOT. Most of our friends are gone, Peter.

ANNE. But we won't forget you.

MARGOT. Ever.

PETER. I'll tell you one thing. When we get out of here, I'm going to make sure no one knows I'm Jewish.

ANNE. *(A strawberry halfway to her mouth, shocked.)* What?

PETER. I'm serious. Life would be a whole lot easier if I were a Christian.

MARGOT. You mean you'd be baptized?

PETER. I don't know. Maybe.

ANNE. I'd never turn away from who I am. I couldn't. Don't you know you'll always be Jewish … in your soul. *(At the foot of the staircase, a dark figure appears, slowly followed by another, then another. A Nazi Officer and two Dutch Collaborators. The first two men have their guns extended, the Third Man, the youngest, carries a black ledger. Soundlessly, they mount the steps. In the attic, Anne, Peter, and Margot keep cleaning and eating the strawberries. Silently, the three men come into the main room, approach the people playing cards. Mr. Dussel sees them first, slowly raises his hands, stands up, dropping the cards. The Franks and the van Daans, realizing what has happened, let their cards fall, raise their hands. The Second Man touches the back of Mrs. Frank's chair. The Annex residents leap to their feet.)*

PETER. *(To Anne.)* I've never seen anything stop you from talking before! *(Grinning, he flicks some water at Anne. Anne flicks some back. Margot joins in. They burst into laughter. The Nazi Officer looks up. Mrs. Frank casts a terrified glance at her husband. The Nazi Officer, his gun raised, starts up the attic steps. The Second Man holds the people downstairs at gunpoint, as the Third Man counts the number of Annex residents in his ledger. The Nazi Officer climbs to the attic, as the laughter continues and we hear Anne voiceover.)*

ANNE. *(V.O.)* It's a wonder I haven't abandoned all my ideals, they seem so absurd and impractical. Yet I cling to them because I still believe, in spite of everything, people are truly good at heart.

NAZI OFFICER. *RAUS!!! (Instantly following "good at heart," his savage scream reverberates as he breaks in on Anne, Margot, and Peter, his gun high. They raise their hands in terror. His scream echoes as he pushes them down the steps. Stumbling, they rush to their parents. The Third Man searches the Frank bedroom for valuables. They stand in two groups — the Frank family in one, the van Daans and Mr. Dussel in the other. Deathly pale, each group huddles together.) LOS!*

NAZI OFFICER and SECOND MAN. *LOS!! (The Franks, the van Daans and Mr. Dussel scatter to their rooms, hurriedly thrust a few belongings into their rucksacks, put on their coats, as the three men ransack the Annex — opening drawers, overturning objects, strewing books and papers over the floor. From utter silence to utter chaos.) SCHNELL! SCHNELL! (In Anne's room, the Third Man rummages through her desk as she stuffs a sweater into her rucksack. Quickly, she grabs her red and white diary from the open desk.)*

THIRD MAN. *(Slapping it out of her hand.) WEG! (Anne stops in her tracks, as the diary clatters to the floor. She reaches for it again, but the Third Man pushes her from the room.)*

ANNE. *(V.O.)* It's utterly impossible to build my life on a foundation of fear. I see the world transformed into a wilderness, I hear the approaching thunder which will destroy us too, I feel the suffering of millions. *(The families are herded out, Mr. Frank and Anne first. Anne clings to her father.)*

NAZI OFFICER. *(Pushing Mr. Frank away from Anne and putting a gun to his head.) JUDENDRECK! SCHNELL! (Going down the steps, Mr. Frank looks back at Anne. She sobs. An animal-like sound. The Nazi Officer pushes her away. She runs to her mother as the Nazi Officer pushes Mr. Dussel, then Peter, down the steps. Mr. van Daan is separated at gunpoint from his wife by the Second Man. Mrs. van Daan reaches for her husband — a desperate silent scream. As Margot, Mrs. Frank and Anne follow, the Third Man seizes the silver music box, lifts the velvet-lined lid. The opening notes of the "Ma'oz Tzur" pour out. Hearing it, Anne turns back. The Third Man shoves her toward the steps, snaps the music box shut, pockets it. The sound of footsteps going down stairs. The sound of a door slamming. The destroyed Annex stares out at us — all life gone. The sound of a police siren. A choked scream merges with the earsplitting sound of a train whistle, the clanking of a rushing train. The sound of the train becomes deafening. Silence. Light comes up on Mr. Frank as he appears in Anne's darkened room in a tattered coat.)*

MR. FRANK. *(Directly to us.)* Westerbork. A barren heath. Wooden towers where our jailers stand guard. Walls covered with thousands of flies. The eight of us crammed into Barrack 67 — betrayed. We never know by whom. Our last month together. *(He pauses.)* Our last month. Anne and Peter walking hand in hand between the barracks and barbed wire. Edith worrying about the children, washing underclothing in murky water, numb. Margot, silent, staring at nothing. Our last days on Dutch soil. *(Pause.)* Late August, Paris freed. Brussels. Antwerp. But for us it is too late. Tuesday September third, 1944, a thousand of us herded into cattle cars, the last transport to leave Westerbork for the extermination camps. *(He pauses.)*

The train. Three days, three nights. In the middle of the third night ... Auschwitz. Separation. Men from women. Edith. Margot. Anne. My family. Never again. Selection. Half our transport killed in the gas chambers. One day Peter and I see a group of men march away, his father among them. Gassed. Peter on the "death march" to Mauthausen. Dead three days before the British arrive. His mother — Auschwitz, Bergen-Belsen, Buchenwald, Theresienstadt — date of death unknown. Mr. Dussel dies in Neuengamme. *(Pause.)*

January twenty-seventh, 1945. I am freed from Auschwitz. I know nothing of Edith and the children. And then I learn ... Edith died in Birkenau of grief, hunger, exhaustion. *(Pause.)*

The winter of '45, typhus breaks out in Bergen-Belsen, killing thousands of prisoners, among them Margot. Anne's friend, Hanneli, sees Anne through the barbed wire, naked, her head shaved, covered with lice. "I don't have anyone anymore," she weeps. A few days later, Anne dies. My daughters' bodies dumped into mass graves, just before the camp is liberated. *(Mr. Frank bends down, picks up Anne's diary lying on the floor. He steps forward, the diary in his hands.)*

All that remains. *(Slowly he opens the diary. The image of Anne's words fills the theatre. Darkness.)*

End of Play

TRANSLATIONS

GERMAN

"Sturmsoldaten"

Ihr Sturmsoldaten jung und alt
nehmt die Waffen in die Hand
Denn der Jude hauset fürchterlich
im deutschen Vaterland

Wenn Sturmsoldat in Schlacht 'rein zieht
ja dann hat er frohen Mut
Wenn das Judenblut vom Messer spritzt
ja geht's nochmal so gut!

You stormtroopers young and old
Take your weapons in your hand
For the dreadful Jew wreaks havoc
In our German fatherland

When the stormtrooper goes into battle
He's full of joyful courage
When Jew-blood spurts from the knife
It's even better yet!

Nazi Broadcast

HITLER. *(V.O.) … und für das wir nun einzutreten entschlossen sind, bis zum letzen Hauch, dieses Deutschland der deutschen Volksgemeinschaft aller deutschen Stämme, das grossdeutsche Reich, Sieg Heil! (As the crowd responds: "Heil!") Sieg Heil! (The crowd screams again: "Heil! Heil!" Ferocious applause. Dead silence.)*

HITLER. *(V.O.)* … and which we are now determined to defend to our last breath, this Germany of the German union of all German tribes, the great German empire, hail victory! *(As the crowd responds: "Hail!")* Hail victory!

"The Horst Wessel Song"

Die Fahne hoch!
Die Reihen fest geschlossen!
SA, marschiert mit ruhig festem Schritt!

The flag on high!
The ranks tightly closed!
The SA marches with quiet steady step!

"Wenn dein Mütterlein"
from Mahler's *Kindertotenlieder*

BROADCAST. *(V.O.)*

Wenn dein Mütterlein
tritt zur Tür herein,
mit der Kerze Schimmer,
ist es mir, als immer
kämst du mit herein,
huschtest hinterdrein,
als wie sonst ins Zimmer!
O du, des Vaters Zelle
Ach, zu schnell
erloschner Freudenschein!

When your mother
appears in the doorway,
in the candlelight,
it's as if
you slipped into the room
beside her,
as you always did.
Oh you, your father's bright spark.
Ah, joy of my life
too quickly extinguished!

HEBREW

("Cha" is not the English "ch" sound, it's the guttural "kha" sound)

Prayers
1.

Sim shalom tova u'vrachah
Chain vo'chesed v'rachamim
Olainu v'al kol yisroel amechoh

Give peace, kindness, and blessing
Life of favor, charity, and mercy
Upon us and all of the house of Israel

2.

Ba-ruch a-ta A-do-nai
E-lo-hei-nu me-lech ha-o-lam
a-sher ki-de-sha-nu be-mits-vo-tav
ve-tsi-va-nu le-had-lik neir
shel Cha-nu-ka.

Praised are You, Adonai our God, Sovereign of the Universe, who makes us holy with mitzvot and instructs us to kindle the lights of Chanuka.

"Ma'oz Tzur"

Ma-oz tzur ye-shu-a-si
Le-cha naw-eh lisha bayah
Ti-kon beis te-fi-la-si
Ve-shum to-daw
n-zaw-bei-ach
L'et takhin matbe'ach
Mitzar hammnabe"

My refuge, my rock of salvation!
'Tis pleasant to sing your praises.
Let our house of prayer be restored.
And there we will offer you our thanks.
When You will have slaughtered the barking foe.
Then we will celebrate with song
And psalm the altar's dedication.

PROPERTY LIST

Playing cards
Cognac and six glasses
Crate of strawberries
Cat in a basket
Umbrella
Large hatbox containing a chamber pot
Satchel
Briefcase
Cigarettes
Silverware
Penknife
Decorated folder with Anne's movie star collection
Diary in red and white checkered cloth
Fountain pen
David Copperfield
Mystery novel
Latin book
French book
Sewing materials
Wooden menorah
Carving knife
Papers
Crocheting materials and wool
Milk
Groceries
Black bag
Cigarette butt
Bulging school bag with:
       manilla envelope
       crossword puzzle book
       bottle filled with green liquid
       cigarette
       slip of paper
       wool scarf
       ball of yarn with ribbons
       little case with razor
       tiny box with earplugs

Small package wrapped in newspaper tied with string containing
    an antique silver music box
Towel
Ficelle (knitted bag) containing red high-heeled shoes
Cake on a plate covered with napkin
Knife
Plates
Supper of kale and potatoes
Comb
Candle
Chunk of bread
Sack of potatoes
Map
Guns
Black ledger and pen

SOUND EFFECTS

The original sound effects created by Dan Moses Schreier for the Broadway production is available through the Play Service, in conjunction with a written performance license of the play. The original effects include:

Pouring rain
Seagulls
Westertoren carillon
Hitler voiceover
Busy office
Door close
Siren
Buzzer
Train whistle
Train rushing by
Voices praying in Hebrew
Planes
Air raid siren
Bombs falling
Machine gun fire
Music box playing the Ma'oz Tzur
Crash
Dog bark
Eisenhower broadcast
Footsteps going down stairs
Door slam
Police siren
Choked scream
Deafening train

The below sound effects should be created by the actors:
Songs: "Sturmsoldaten" and "The Horst Wessel Song"
BBC Radio Free Europe broadcasts
Bolkestein (Dutch Minister of Education) voiceover
Rauter (SS Chief of the occupied Netherlands) voiceover

NOTES
(Use this space to make notes for your production)

NOTES
(Use this space to make notes for your production)

NOTES
(Use this space to make notes for your production)

NOTES
(Use this space to make notes for your production)

NOTES
(Use this space to make notes for your production)

NOTES
(Use this space to make notes for your production)

NOTES

(Use this space to make notes for your production)

NOTES

(Use this space to make notes for your production)

NOTES
(Use this space to make notes for your production)

NOTES
(Use this space to make notes for your production)

NOTES
(Use this space to make notes for your production)